LOVE IN ACTION

HEALING CON·FLICT
IN YOUR CHURCH

LOVE
IN
ACTION

ROBERT MOELLER
FOREWORD BY MARSHALL SHELLEY

MULTNOMAH BOOKS

LOVE IN ACTION
©1994 by Robert Moeller

Published by Multnomah Books
a part of the Questar Publishing Family

Edited by Rodney L. Morris
Cover design by David Carlson

Printed in the United States of America

International Standard Book Number 0-88070-672-4

To my wife Cheryl
To our four children
To our friends in the local church

LOVE IN ACTION - Robert MOELLER.

Contents

Foreword

A few years ago, I discovered the power of nuance and naming. I was writing a book on conflict in the church—specifically on people who seemed to be the sources of tension, time after time. A surprising pattern quickly emerged from the dozens of interviews with pastors and key lay leaders: In most cases, the problem people didn't intend to be difficult. They sincerely thought they were doing what was right. Their well-meaning motives, however, were lost in the turbulence they created by their abrasive attitudes, cutting comments, or rigid resistance toward anything that wasn't on their agendas. These people left ulcers, discouragement, and broken relationships in their wakes. How are we to love these people without giving in to their negativism?

At lunch one day, a church leader said, "These people are well-intentioned dragons." The phrase clicked. *That's exactly it*, I thought. In three words, he captured the complexity and the fear of the situation I'd been trying to describe. It's no surprise that *Well-Intentioned Dragons* became the name of that book.

Bob Moeller is a kindred spirit. He is a perceptive observer of people, with an amazingly accurate intuition of their motivations, dreams, and fears. He identifies and interprets significant nuances. Then he helpfully names the situation, allowing us to respond in a wise and God-honoring way.

Besides that, Bob is one of the best storytellers I know. His ability to notice detail and appreciate the humor in even dark situations makes him an astute author and insightful guide for all of us who want to lead our churches to significant ministry done in the Spirit of Christ.

Love is not a sentiment we pour over our daily activities like some sticky syrup. No, love is a skill, a wise use of our abilities to bring out the best in others and help them to experience God in a life-changing way.

Even in painful and stress-filled conflict, "they will know we are Christians by our love." This book points us to that deeply ingrained and streetwise love. It better equips us to put *Love in Action*.

Marshall Shelley
Executive Editor
Leadership Journal

Acknowledgments

I wish to thank the numerous individuals who contributed generously of their time and wisdom to this book. In particular, my thanks to H. B. London, Speed Leas, Norman Shawchuck, Carl George, Paul Cedar, Robert Page, Dean Johnson, Thomas McDill, and the other pastors and lay leaders who granted interviews. Their insights, wisdom, and years of experience significantly impacted the course of this book.

I also wish to express my appreciation to Kevin Miller, Marshall Shelley, and the entire staff at *Leadership Journal* for granting permission to use a variety of materials. As friends, colleagues, and fellow journalists, they are wonderful people to know and work with.

My thanks as well to my wife Cheryl, a gifted editor and my best friend. Her advice and counsel has been of enormous value in the production of this book. She and our four children are sure evidence of the love and grace God has poured out on my life.

Finally, my thanks to the people at Questar Publishers for their support and backing of this project. In particular, my thanks to Rod Morris who did the insightful work of editing the manuscript and preparing it for publication. To all the associates at this remarkable company, thank you for your desire to strengthen the local church to be Christ's hands and feet in this world.

Preface

I grew up in a neighborhood where I was one of the older kids on the block. On one occasion, several of us decided to help our little red-headed neighbor, David, learn how to ride his new bike.

We went over with him the fundamentals of peddling, steering, and keeping his balance. David seemed to learn quickly. After several trial runs, it was decided he was at last ready to go it alone.

Because we lived on a street with a slope, it was an ideal place to give him the momentum he needed. We walked the bike up to the top of the street. David bravely climbed on, nodded at us, and in a moment of high drama, we sent him on his way. His balance was shaky, the bike veered this way, then that way, but David held on. We all cheered as David careened from one side of the street to the other. He was doing it—David was riding a bike all on his own!

He was half way down the street when a sobering thought hit me: I hadn't taught David how to use his brakes. As David picked up speed, his look of triumph turned to one of terror. He was headed straight for the edge of a five-foot bank that went straight down into a swamp.

"Whoa..." is the last thing we heard David say as he disappeared over the edge.

We were breathless when we arrived at the edge of the bank

to see what had happened to David. "Are you all right?" we yelled. There David lay in the weeds, his bike wheels spinning in the air, a dazed smile on his face. He was a bit shaken, but at least no bones had been broken.

What had gone wrong? David had climbed onto a vicious cycle he didn't know how to stop.

Much the same thing can be said about many local churches today. As forced dismissals, group schisms, and short tenures of pastors become more common, one may get the feeling many congregations are peddling a vicious cycle they don't know how to stop. Once conflict gets going, things soon reach the point where they are out of control.

This book contains the stories of individuals and churches who have been on the hair-raising ride through serious church conflict. Names, locations, denominational affiliations, and other details have been altered to protect confidentiality. Chapters 1, 3, 5, and 13 are fictional, but illustrate principles that are true of many church conflicts. Chapters 9, 10, and 11 are based on true situations, but the names and places have been changed.

This book is written in the confidence that God's plan for each believer includes sacrificial and joyful participation in the local church. It is also written in the conviction that God has something better for us as believers than division and acrimony. Like any family, it pleases the heart of our Father to see his children obey him and love one another deeply.

Love in Action does not offer the final answers to solving church conflict. Local church conflict is an often complex problem, requiring a variety of solutions. Simplistic answers rarely work.

But if local churches take to heart the principles and steps recommended—and live them out in a spirit of faith, hope, and love—they can be spared the experience of going over the edge.

PART 1

When the Family Feuds

CHAPTER 1

A Father's Will

L et's get this thing over with so we can go home," muttered
Krista under her breath.

"Calm down, sweetheart," said Jeff, her husband. "It's
impolite to be in a hurry at a funeral. Besides, your mother needs
you."

The two glanced toward an older woman, who stared in grief
and silent contemplation at her husband's walnut-colored casket.
It had all happened so quickly. One hour he was out in the garden,
robust, laughing, getting things ready for spring planting. The next
he was strapped to a stretcher with an oxygen mask over his face.
He died before any of his children could reach his bedside.

"I can't believe Tommy. How does he have the gall to bring
her to something like this?" whispered Krista.

Jeff looked at Krista's younger brother, Tom, who stood next
to his mother and his second wife, Anne. Tom had met Anne at
work soon after he had been released from treatment for cocaine
abuse. Tom was the sort who never let on with his feelings, particularly in front of his family. He wore a blank expression as he
gazed at his father's body.

Tommy's two children from his previous marriage had come to the wake. They looked nervous as they sat next to their cousins. The boy and girl were old enough to grieve, but still too young to tell anyone how much they were going to miss Grandpa Ted. Since Tommy had left them, Grandpa Ted had become to them a second father. Tommy's first wife had recently remarried. She decided the funeral was one family event she would miss, so she sent the children with their father.

"I can't stand him," Krista said.

"Tommy has a right to be here," Jeff said. "After all, Ted was his father too."

"Yeah, and dad might have lived longer if Tommy hadn't pulled all his antics. He should be ashamed to even show his face here."

Tommy happened to glance in Krista's direction. She looked down to keep from making eye contact. But she knew Jeff was right—this wasn't the time or the place to settle old scores. That would have to wait.

"I think I'm going to go see how Jenna's doing. She seems to be taking this awfully hard," said Krista. She walked over to the front row of blue velvet-covered seats in the funeral chapel. Jenna, her younger sister, was curled over, and her shoulders shook as she cried.

"Hey, how's my little sister?" Krista said as she sat down.

"I miss him so much already," said Jenna. "I never even got a chance to say..." She wasn't able to finish her sentence. She broke down into loud sobbing. Others in the room turned away from their quiet conversations to look her way. Most politely resumed their small talk.

Krista leaned closer and stroked her sister's hair. "There, there, you're going to be all right," she said.

"No, I'm not," Jenna said. She had left home at eighteen and moved to the West Coast to attend college. It was more to escape than to attend a good school. Tired of the tension in her family, she rarely came home for vacations or holidays. Most of her life she had played the rebel. No one was surprised when she decided to get married without telling them.

But when she finally did bring Bryan home with her, the welcome was less than enthusiastic. Only one day into the visit, she and her younger brother, Phillip, had gotten into a shouting match in the kitchen.

"Hey, I hear Bryan dropped out of college," Phillip had said. "I hear there's a great future in managing car washes."

"You irresponsible, spoiled brat," shouted Jenna. "No one ever wanted you in the first place."

"Get lost, sister. No one cares whether you come or go. No one even considers you part of this family any more."

After that incident, Jenna had stayed away for the next two years.

Born several years after Jenna, Phillip was still single and in college. He stood in the corner of the chapel with his roommates and discussed baseball. He really didn't care about baseball that day, but the last thing he wanted to do was cry in front of anyone.

As he looked at his father's lifeless face, he wanted to know just one thing: "Did you really want me, Dad? Or was Jenna right?" It was not only Jenna who considered him a nuisance; Krista had taken her shots at him through the years, too.

After Krista married, she would often come home and complain, "Why don't you make Phil do the work around here we had to do when we were growing up?"

"Phillip does his share," his mother would say.

"Sure he does."

Phillip would overhear these conversations and privately seethe at his older sister. On one occasion he had finally had enough. He burst into the room and shouted, "Why don't you shut up, Krista! You're not my mother."

Their mother rarely did much to stop their sibling rivalry. "Really, you two," she would say, "I wish you would learn to get along." Despite all the hard feelings between Phil and his sisters, he had secretly longed to be their friend.

Ted was the only force that had held the family together in recent years. He would often plead with his children in private to get along, but the truces always proved to be temporary.

But now he was gone, and with his departure went the glue to keep the family from flying apart permanently. Phil wondered if he'd ever see Jenna or Tommy again once the funeral was over. They both lived out of state and only came home when his dad would call and invite them.

Now, Dad would never call anyone again.

"Could I see the immediate family in the next room?" asked Pastor Jennings in a quiet voice. It was 9:00 P.M. and the reviewal was nearly over.

Jenna had regained her composure by this time, so Krista got up and rejoined her husband next to a spray of white flowers. "Stay close to me," she whispered, "We haven't all been in one room together for years. Who knows what may happen."

"Just relax, honey," whispered Jeff. "It's going to be fine."

Pastor Jennings, a middle-aged man with slightly graying hair and a natural smile, pointed the family toward a private conference room off to the side of the chapel. It took a few minutes for the entire group to assemble in the room as friends and relatives stopped each one and offered a final hug and word of condolence. Once everyone was seated in a semicircle, Pastor Jennings closed the door.

"I know this is a terribly difficult hour for you," he said. "Ted was a wonderful man. Just as you have lost a father or a husband or a brother, I have lost a good friend. I shall miss Ted..." The pastor's voice broke ever so slightly in the middle of the sentence.

"Please, excuse me," he said, "I'm the one who's supposed to be comforting you."

Tommy's wife, Anne, an attractive woman who wore pain in her eyes, never looked up. She could feel the animosity directed toward her by several of the family members. She had come to the wake only because she was afraid Tommy wouldn't make it on his own. She knew that if the stress level got too high, and there was no one to help him, he might go back to his cocaine problem.

Tommy glanced at Jenna, and a well of emotions came up inside. *You've always hated me*, he thought to himself. *From the time I was born, all I remember is you putting me down and telling me I was stupid.*

His sister's face was hard. All the cosmetics she wore that day couldn't veil her deeply etched bitterness.

He glanced toward Krista, then at her husband. *I pity you, Jeff. What is it like to live with someone who believes she's perfect? Control, sister. That's what you're all about. Controlling everyone and everything about you.*

"So we find Jesus' great promise in John 14," said Pastor Jennings. He thumbed through his pocket-sized Bible and adjusted his half-glasses to help him read the fine print, "Do not let your hearts be troubled. Trust in God; trust also in me. In my Father's house are many rooms; if it were not so, I would have told you. I am going there to prepare a place for you. And if I go and prepare a place for you, I will come back and take you to be with me that you also may be where I am."

Pastor Jennings took off his glasses and began to explain the importance of heaven in an hour like this.

At least where Dad is he doesn't have to hear mom complain anymore, thought Jenna. Jenna had always loved her father. She secretly sided with him when her mother would berate him. Once, when she was fourteen, she interrupted one of their arguments and said, "Mom, why don't you just lay off Dad? All you ever do is criticize him. Give the man some space."

Her mother exploded and refused to speak to her for three days. Eventually she made Jenna apologize, though Jenna didn't mean a word of her retraction. That's when Jenna finally decided she would get out of the house at the first opportunity.

"Shall we pray?" said the pastor. Everyone looked down, everyone except Phillip. He didn't feel like praying. His dad was gone. He didn't want to talk to the Person who had taken his dad away.

Phillip was the only child in the family who had refused to go to church in junior high and high school. His parents had decided to let him make up his own mind on the matter. That aggravated Krista, who had been made to attend each and every Sunday service from the time she was born.

"You spoiled brat," she would say when they were alone. "You have Mom and Dad wrapped around your finger."

"Lord, we are drawn close to one another for comfort and strength in this hour of sorrow," Pastor Jennings prayed. "Help us to carry each other's burden of grief, to offer the comfort that a loving family can offer one another."

Yeah, right, thought Phillip to himself. *You're from the moon, Pastor.*

Margaret looked around the room at her children. *I wonder if I'm going to be left alone now?* she thought. She studied the face of each of her children and tried hard not to think about the regrets each represented. A deep, dull pain seared her soul.

She regretted how she had treated her husband the morning of his heart attack. "Don't talk to me until you're ready to say you're sorry!" she had shouted at him.

Ted had decided to go out to the garden to let her blow off steam. It was a tactic he had used with her many times. She had refused to make him lunch that day, a small punishment to be sure, but one that effectively communicated her ongoing anger.

Margaret had been raised in a tumultuous and unstable family. She had married Ted thinking it would bring her the love and stability she had never known as a youngster. Instead, she carried into her marriage her parent's penchant for anger and verbal abuse.

"I'm sorry, Ted," she prayed quietly. "I'm so sorry. If only I had known this was going to happen. I loved you. I really did..." She took out a handkerchief and began to cry.

The day of the funeral came and went with little to distinguish it from other sad farewells. The family sat next to each other at the graveside. The pastor offered a few final words, and then prayed. Friends and relatives walked over and said what they could to be of comfort.

As the family got up to leave, there were a few, brief moments of unrestrained emotion and tears. But while there were tears, there was very little feeling. One or two of the siblings hugged each other, but they quickly broke off their embraces.

The funeral luncheon was noisy and unnatural, as most funeral luncheons are. Pent-up emotions had to be released, and in this culture it's done over small sandwiches and carbonated punch. Only Jenna and Krista sat next to each other, and two hours later, the ordeal was over.

There was only one awkward item of business left to be accomplished—the reading of the will. Once that was over, everyone would be free to retreat into their isolated world of self-interest. Back home, away from the scent of funeral flowers and fresh earth, they could put the difficult events, and the difficult people, of the last four days behind them—forever.

"Mr. Barnaby will see you now," smiled the paralegal assistant. A pleasant woman in her early thirties, she stood in the waiting room of the law firm of Savowitz, Barnaby, and Nagele. It was crowded and humid in the small entry room.

"At last," said Phillip, dressed in shorts and a tee shirt. "This place gives me claustrophobia."

"You didn't need to dress up for the occasion," said Krista. Phil glared back at his sister. The temperature in the room seemed to go up another three degrees.

"Hey, I'm with Phil," interrupted Jeff, trying to sound conciliatory. "I've sweat off two pounds in the last twenty minutes."

"I never did have any time for this place," complained the mother. "But you're father insisted on doing all his business here. He never would listen to me about anything."

"Can we go easy on Dad for just a day?" Jenna asked. "Besides, Bryan and I have a 2:00 P.M. flight back to L.A. All I care about is getting out of here."

Margaret looked hurt by her daughter's comment, but decided not to say anything. The family was ushered into an elegant conference room, complete with a polished mahogany table and expensive leather chairs.

"Is the entire family here, Mrs. Swanson?" asked the sixty-year-old attorney.

"Yes," she said.

"Good, then if it's acceptable with you, we'll get on with the matter at hand."

"I'm all for that," sighed Phillip, who crossed his arms and pushed back from the table.

The distinguished lawyer smiled his direction. He was used to moments such as this. Moments where money and grief coincide. The one question on everyone's mind was usually, "What do I get out of this?"

"My husband and I have to catch a plane," Jenna said. "Our cab is due here in thirty minutes. Will we get this over in time?"

"Can't wait to get out of town again?" Tommy asked.

Everyone turned his direction in disbelief. It was the first time he had said anything in the last three days. He was even surprised by what he had just said. Jenna started to get up.

Here it comes, thought Phil. He looked at Jenna's red face and braced himself for the counterattack.

"Cool it, Tommy," said Krista. Bryan shot Tommy a leave-her-alone-or-you'll-answer-to-me stare.

"Just kidding," Tommy mumbled. He smirked to himself and looked down at the floor again. Jenna relaxed and sat back down in her chair.

"The sooner we let Mr. Barnaby conclude his business, the sooner we can all go home," said the mother. She turned toward the attorney, "Please proceed."

The lawyer opened a file folder that had an elastic band around it. He pulled out what looked like at least an inch of papers.

"You're going to read all that?" Phillip said. "We'll be here till supper."

"No, Phil," chuckled the lawyer. "These are duplicate copies of your father's last will and testament. I'll give you each a copy at the conclusion of our session."

Phil's faux pas allowed a moment of comic relief.

"When's the last time you read anything, Phil?" Jenna asked. "Too bad it isn't on video for you."

"Shut up," he said in a half-serious voice.

"What's this?" asked Krista. She was seated next to the attorney and picked up her copy of the will. At the end of document were stapled five pages of a different color. She held it up and flipped back to the end section. "My Final Words to My Family," she read out loud.

"Oh, I'm glad you've noticed, Krista," Mr. Barnaby said. "What you're pointing to is an addendum to your father's will that he brought in last fall, just after Thanksgiving."

The word *Thanksgiving* made Jenna and Tommy a little uncomfortable. Both had skipped the event. Jenna hadn't even called that day. Tommy had spent the day with his new wife's parents.

"Ted never told me he did anything like that," said the widow. "But then again, he liked to keep me in the dark about most things."

Jenna was about to say something but her husband squeezed her hand under the table. She looked at him and he shook his head.

"We'll get to that portion of the will in just a few minutes," said the attorney. "But let's begin at the top of page one." He cleared his throat and started to read, "I, Theodore John Swanson, being of sound mind and body..."

There wasn't much of anything out of the ordinary in the main document. The father had bequeathed all his property and assets to his wife, and upon her death the remainder of the estate was to be divided equally among the four children. He did, however, designate that the funds from one of his life insurance policies be distributed immediately to the children. That clause seemed to catch the interest of everyone in the room.

"After taxes, Mr. Barnaby, how much will each of the children receive?" asked the widow.

"Assuming a 23 percent tax bracket or so, Mrs. Swanson, I'd guess about thirty-five thousand dollars," said the attorney.

That should be enough to support Tommy's habit for about a month, thought Krista. *I'd like to own a red BMW. No, I'll add a great room to our home.*

"Mr. Swanson did stipulate one precondition to the distribution of the gift," said the attorney. Suddenly all eyes in the room locked in his direction.

"What do you mean 'precondition,' Mr. Barnaby?" Jenna asked.

"Yeah, say that in English," said Phillip. He could already see himself on the slopes of the Alps enjoying the ultimate European skiing vacation.

"That will become clear as we get to the addendum," Barnaby said. "If you have no more questions about the main document, why don't we turn to the last section."

That their portion of the estate might be in jeopardy over-rode the siblings' normal reluctance to look one another in the eye. Now they all exchanged concerned looks with each other. Each of them wanted their money—and with no hassle.

"As I said earlier, Ted brought this document in last November," said Barnaby. "He had written it out in long-hand and asked that I include it in his last will and testament."

"Maybe Daddy had some type of premonition or something," said Jenna. "You know, you read about people getting things together just before they..." The image of the pallbearers carrying her father's coffin out of the chapel came back full force. She bit her lip as tears welled in her eyes.

"It's okay, honey," said Bryan. "You'll get over it."

"I'm not sure I want to get over it," she said, her hand covering her eyes.

"I don't want to sound unsympathetic, but we are wasting Mr. Barnaby's time," said Krista in an older sister voice. It was clear someone needed to take control of the situation.

"Yes, let's get on with it," said the widow.

"Friday, November 28," the lawyer began. "Today, as I sit down to write this letter, I do so after celebrating my sixty-ninth Thanksgiving. I am feeling in good health, my spirits are strong, and I look forward to celebrating several more holidays with the family I love so much."

Tommy looked away.

"But life is uncertain, and today's bright sun can quickly

become tomorrow's dark storm. So while I still have the presence of mind and health to do so, I am writing a letter to each of you, the people I love more than anyone else—my dear wife, Margaret; my four children, Krista, Thomas, Jenna, and Phillip, their husbands and wives; and of course, my seven wonderful grandchildren."

He still loves me? thought Tommy. His wife, sensing the significance of the moment, took her husband's hand.

"I want to say something to each of you I was unable to say during my lifetime, either because I lacked the words or the courage to do so. Or perhaps it was because we all simply became too busy to share our hearts with one another.

"Let me begin with my oldest daughter, Krista."

Krista could feel her stomach tighten. This was much more intimate than she cared for. The situation was suddenly beyond her control, a feeling she dreaded.

"Krista, you were the first miracle to enter our lives. In fact, you were born the day of a terrible blizzard. I was making minimum wage working as a night custodian. Your mother and I were both trying to finish college and we never knew where our next meal was going to come from. But let me assure you, you were no expense to us. The day you were born I danced down the hallway with my broom."

Krista laughed out loud and the others laughed with her. Her husband reached over and rubbed his wife's back. The lawyer looked at her and smiled. He then continued to read. "But two years later, when Thomas was born, you weren't so sure you liked someone else invading your domain."

You can say that again, thought Tommy.

"I still remember the day Margaret and I caught you standing in Tommy's crib, jumping up and down on top of him. It nearly scared your mother and me to death. But later, when we told friends about the incident, they laughed till they cried. Eventually we did, too."

"You still have the footprints on your chest, Tommy?" Phillip asked, trying to sound lighthearted.

"Yeah, I still have the scars," he said, half-smiling.

The lawyer continued, "Krista, recently I realized that I was letting life slip by without telling you something very important. It was always my hunch that the day we brought Thomas home, you felt you had to divide our love with him. You were wrong, my darling girl. We didn't divide our love that day for either of you. We doubled it."

For a moment Krista and Tommy's eyes met.

"Krista, may I leave this last request with you? Give up once and for all resenting Tommy. He never meant you any harm. He only wanted your approval."

There was a palpable tension in the air. Everyone sat perfectly still around the table.

"He wanted to be your friend, Krista. Do something I wish you had done the day he came home with us—reach out and welcome him into the family. He belongs to you, and you belong to him. Experience the joy of his friendship. It's still not too late, at least I trust it is not too late."

Krista swallowed hard. She reached in her purse for a Kleenex. Tommy shifted in his chair.

"I don't know what he's talking about," said the widow. "Tommy and Krista always got along fine. Mr. Barnaby, would you please continue. Ted was always imagining there were problems when there wasn't."

Not only had the mother never confronted the sibling rivalry at home, at times she found it worked to her advantage. As long as all her children had a common enemy in each other, she could be the common ally of all. It was a strategy she had seen her mother use effectively growing up.

"Of course, Mrs. Swanson, as you wish," said the attorney. Phillip banged his shoe against the table as he shifted in his seat.

"Thomas, I trust you're present today as well. Tommy, I suspect you were the sensitive one of the family. You were the artist, and like all artists, you felt things deeply." Tears started to gather in Anne's eyes as she looked at her troubled husband.

"From the time you were old enough to walk, you ran from the television when violent or frightening programs came on. You seemed to have a compassion for the entire world. One day, when you were five, you found a bird in the backyard that had broken its wing. I remember you carried it inside and insisted I take it to the hospital. Later that night, when it died, you cried yourself to sleep. Life was always difficult for you, Tommy, because you never wanted to see anyone get hurt."

"Why did he put things like this in a letter anyway?" mumbled Mrs. Swanson. She started to fiddle with something in her purse. The lawyer thought it best to continue reading.

"Tommy, I don't know why you chose to do some of the things you did in college and afterward. Maybe it was to try and wash away hurts too difficult to bear. Maybe it was a search for love. But you chose to run from life."

Tommy gestured as if he was about to get up from the table. His wife reached over and whispered something in his ear. He grimaced for a moment, then decided to hear his father out.

"Tommy, I'm gone now, but there's something I want you to know. Nothing you have ever done, nor anything you will ever do, will change my love for you. It's permanent, unchangeable, eternal. If you're wondering if I've forgiven you, then let me settle that question right here and now. I have forgiven you—of everything. Not only for the past, but for the future. It's a done deal, son, and you can't undo it. My final request is this, Tommy: Come home. Krista, Jenna, Phillip, welcome your brother home. It's time for all of you to be a family."

Tommy felt as though he was going to explode on the inside.

"Would anyone like coffee or something cold to drink?" the

paralegal poked her head inside the door. Everyone was so glad for the interruption that they could have hugged the woman.

"I'd like some iced tea if you have some," said Jenna in an unnaturally cheerful voice.

"Do you have any Coke?" Phil asked. "It's hot in here."

The next few minutes were spent taking orders for drinks. Several people got up and excused themselves to step outside for a moment. About ten minutes later, it was clear they were going to have to hurry if Jenna and Bryan were to catch their plane.

"I don't know if I can go back in there," said Jenna to her husband. "Our family has never dealt with these kinds of issues before. My therapist said we aren't ready to be this honest with each other—not yet. This is going to cause another huge blow-up, just mark my words."

"Are you sure you just aren't afraid of what he's going to say about you?" asked Bryan.

"Maybe."

"Look, honey, Barnaby said there's something at the end of your dad's will that affects us getting the money. Can you hang in there just another few minutes? Then we can go home and never come back if we don't feel like it."

"I suppose, but if it gets too heavy, I'm out of there."

The group shuffled into the room and reconvened.

"There's just another page or two to go," Barnaby said.

"Good deal," sighed Phillip.

"I continue on page six," said Barnaby. "To my sweetheart, Jenna. Ah yes, you were born with a strong will, my beautiful daughter. If you had been a boy, I would have considered naming you Jacob instead, after the character who wrestled with God in the book of Genesis. From the moment you were born, you wrestled with your mother and me. It's like you wanted to crawl out of your crib and take on the world."

"She did," said Krista. Everyone laughed but Jenna, who pretended not to hear.

"It seems like you and I had a number of wrestling matches through the years, Jenna. The issues changed as the years did, but you continued your struggle. But this much you need to know. Regardless of how many times we argued, fought, and misunderstood one another, you were always my little girl. Nothing could or ever has changed that."

Jenna looked out the office window and thought she saw a yellow cab pull into the parking lot.

"My last request of you is that you allow me to bless you, Jenna. Like the Lord, who blessed Jacob at the end of the match, so I bestow my love, approval, and favor upon your life, as I do upon all my other children listening to this letter. Please, stop wrestling, stop fighting. There are people who wish to love you, embrace you. But you have to let them. Do me this last favor, Jenna. Accept the family God gave you, even with all its faults and imperfections. Open your heart to them. Nothing would make me happier."

"Is there a cab out there, Mr. Barnaby?" Bryan asked. The attorney put down the paper and glanced out the window.

"I believe there is," he said.

"I really hate to interrupt this, but Jenna and I—"

"Wait, Bryan," Jenna said. "I want to hear the rest of what Daddy had to say."

"But, sweetheart, it's at least thirty minutes to the airport, and we have to pick up Megan."

"I said I wanted to stay."

"Okay. Have it your way," Bryan said.

"I'll try and hurry," said the attorney. "There's just a few paragraphs left." By this time Mrs. Swanson was fanning herself with a bulletin from the service the day before.

"Phillip, my youngest," said the attorney. "You were the final gift of heaven to Margaret and me. We had been parents many years by the time you arrived. I know you must have wondered at times, particularly during your teenage years, if you were a so-called 'accident.' Son, there are no accidents when it comes to children. You were born of love, and God intended you to be a part of our lives as much as any of your brothers and sisters."

Krista searched through her purse for an aspirin. She could feel the tension in the back of her neck. Phillip sat motionless, any movement on his part and he felt he might lose it.

"Phillip, as of the day I write this letter, to my knowledge you still have not found your life's mate. If I should leave this earth before you do find her, my passing will no doubt be a lonely and difficult transition for you. Unlike your brothers and sisters, you will have no mate to bear your sorrows with you. So turn to the people God has given you, son. Turn to Krista, Jenna, Tommy, and your mother.

"Children, Phillip needs you. Welcome him into your hearts, despite the age and other differences between you. Help carry him through this time. The season for rejection is over. It must be."

Phil had managed until now to hold it all together, but it was impossible to do so any longer. He put his head down on the table and began to sob.

"Be strong, Phillip," said his mother. "It's a hard time for all of us."

"Let him cry," said Krista.

Phillip couldn't believe his ears. In his twenty-one years he had never remembered his sister once offer a kind word to him. Then, in a moment of sacred silence, she reached her hand across the table and he took it.

To everyone's astonishment, Tommy got up next. He went over to his younger brother and hugged him. He began to cry as well. Jenna sat there, the ropes of her strong will unraveling by the moment.

The horn of the cab sounded twice in the parking lot. Jenna

looked out the window, looked at the trio of her brothers and sister embracing, then turned to her husband.

"Tell the cab to leave," she whispered.

"What?"

"I'm not going, not today," she said.

"But our tickets are nonrefundable," Bryan pleaded.

Jenna ignored him, got up from the table, and went over to her mother. She knelt down next to the woman, who had no idea what she should do next.

"Mom," Jenna said, "I want...I want to end the match—today."

Her mother, terrified, yet broken by what she was witnessing around the table, let out a loud cry, then embraced her daughter.

"I'm so sorry for the mean things I've done to you," Jenna said.

Jeff and Bryan, left sitting at the table, looked at one another and shook their heads in disbelief.

"I forgive you, sweetheart," stammered her mother.

"Perhaps, we should take a recess," said Barnaby, who was forced to wipe tears from his own eyes.

"Read the rest," said Krista, who let go of Phillip's hand. "We need to hear it."

"Very well," the attorney said. "I shall do my best to get through it." He picked up the document. "In closing, let me say to my dear wife, Margaret, if I had it to do all over again, I would choose you as my wife again, and again, and again. You were my closest friend, my most ardent supporter, and the person I loved most in this life. Thank you for the gift of these years. I shall miss you. I shall wait for you."

The attorney and Margaret smiled at one another through their tears.

"In conclusion, to receive the allotment I have designated to each of you, I place only one precondition. You must simply say to one another, 'For our father's sake, I love you, I forgive you, and I accept you.'"

The next day a small group of people stood around the fresh grave of Ted Swanson. They placed a wreath on top of it, with a short note inside. It read, "Dear Dad, your will has been done on earth, as you wished from heaven." It was signed by all four children.

They stood together on that windswept hill and cried. Then, when tears had done their good work, they walked away, arm in arm.

CHAPTER 2

How to Break
a Father's Heart

One of the dangers of being a parent is that your kids can cause you pain. Adults who have raised children can tell you it's an occupational hazard.

I once visited a man who was only days away from death. The hospital had sent him home to spend his final hours in familiar surroundings. When we got onto the topic of his children, his expression changed from pleasant and cheerful to one of anguish and pain.

"Bob, all my children are grown now. I had hoped that as adults they might become better friends. Instead, it seems they are always finding something to fight about."

I suspect that somehow his sad expression mirrors the sorrow in the face of our Father when he looks down and sees his children bicker and argue with one another.

There is something terribly wrong, even unnatural, about a family that is at war with itself. That's particularly true when that family is the family of God found in the local church. No human father can watch his children belittle, attack, and say hateful things to one another without feeling deep and profound grief.

Imagine how much more sorrow the perfect heart of our heavenly Father feels when he sees his children clash and war with one another in the church.

THE CHURCH AT WAR

A pastor stood outside his New England church one bright, summer morning, and greeted children as they bounced along on their way to Sunday school.

The pastor extended his hand to one of the children, "How are you, Karin?" he said to a sweet, six-year-old girl.

"My mommy says she hates you," she replied matter-of-factly.

The pastor was momentarily stunned by the little girl's remark. "But...why?" he mumbled. "Why does she hate me?"

"Because she says you've ruined the church," she said, sincerity shining through her big brown eyes. "Both my daddy and my mommy say they wish you would leave."

A church could not agree on who to call as their next pastor. The group was split between two candidates. Unable to reconcile their differences, each faction dug in their heels. The division reached a crisis point when both groups extended a call to their favorite candidate. Incredibly, both men accepted the job, and both arrived to preach their first sermon on the same day. Each preacher tried to gain the attention of the audience by talking over the other, and it wasn't long until an argument broke out in the congregation. It escalated into a fist-fight in the center aisle. The police had to be summoned to break up the melee, and the service canceled to avoid the possibility of further violence. "Onward Christian Soldiers" took on an entirely new meaning that morning.

The pastor put down the phone in disbelief. He had just received word that his only daughter had been killed in a car accident in another state. The same day, numb and grief-stricken, he was forced to board a plane and travel to a distant city to begin making the necessary funeral arrangements.

The next day, when he first viewed his lifeless daughter lying in a casket, it was too much for him. He bent over and wept, certain he could not go on with life. But somehow he managed to survive that day, and the next. Then came the day of the funeral. As he scanned the flowers arranged by the coffin, he was surprised to see that no note or floral arrangement had arrived from his church.

Following the funeral, still in the daze of shock and grief, he made the long journey back to his home church. He knew he would have to somehow try and pick up the pieces of his shattered life.

That's when he received the call that sent him over the edge.

"Pastor," said one of his church officers on the other end of the line, "The board has decided to dock you a week's vacation for the time you were gone."

"You...you can't be serious," he said.

"I am," came the reply. "We had to pay someone to preach while you were away."

That day a bruised reed was broken in two. The pastor resigned from his church and left the ministry.

A Time of Colliding Thunderheads

I wish these three stories were isolated instances of division and conflict in the local church, but they are not. While the circumstances are unique to each situation, the problem of painful, divisive, and unloving behavior in the family of God is all too common.

If it were possible to use spiritual radar to gain a graphic view of the condition of the church in North America today, you would see huge weather systems and thunderheads colliding with one another. In three-dimensional computer enhanced imagery, you would observe massive upper air turbulence creating violent lightning storms, terrifying straight-line winds, and deadly cyclones and tornadoes spinning across the land.

But from our limited, human perspective, we can't see these storm fronts crashing into one another. They're invisible. What we can see instead is a sanctuary half-empty on a Sunday morning because one faction got angry at another and left to start another church.

Or we walk by a pastor's office and notice his bookshelves are empty and his desk bare as pavement. He was terminated by the board with little or no warning.

Or perhaps we might catch a glimpse of a wounded volunteer sitting alone at the back of a sanctuary. She was just told she isn't needed any longer. A younger, more politically savvy person is going to replace her. It might have been time for a change, but the way it was done left her devastated.

Whether the conflict is between the pastor and the congregation, the pastor and the board, or between one member and another, if not managed properly, the result is a wounded body of believers. Wounds that can prove fatal to a local church.

President James Garfield was shot in the back by an assassin near the end of the nineteenth century. While seriously injured, he miraculously survived the attack. Despite their best efforts, physicians were not able to locate the bullet. They probed for days and days, trying to find it.

Eventually, the president died. Some believe it wasn't the bullet that cost him his life. It is more likely he died of the infection caused by the continuous probing and reopening of the wound. When church conflict is allowed to fester and wounds are never effectively healed, the body becomes diseased and suffers. If resentment, bitterness, and unforgiveness are allowed to infect the congregation, the condition can become terminal.

The weekly worship services may yet go on, the lawn may

still get mowed, and someone might even stand in the pulpit to preach each Sunday, but the church is effectively dead.

The True Scandal of Our Time

A friend of ours sold encyclopedias door to door in California. She was following up on a phone lead and came to the second floor of an apartment building. She knocked on the door, and the man opened it. She gulped. She could see from the emblem on his leather jacket that he belonged to a notorious motorcycle gang.

She thought about leaving, but his polite manner and genuine interest in her product persuaded her to stay. He invited her to come into the living room and make her presentation. As she walked in, she noticed another member of the gang happened to be there. She made her sales pitch, but was constantly interrupted by the second gang member.

"Shut up," the first gang member said to his friend. "I want to hear what she has to say." But he continued to make snide and impolite remarks to our friend.

"You'll have to excuse me," said the first gang member. He went over to his obnoxious friend, dragged him out to the balcony of his apartment—and threw him over the side.

Our friend was horrified, but managed to remain calm. When the gang member casually took his place on the sofa again, he said, "I apologize for the interruption. Please, go on."

While motorcycle gang members aren't known for their kind affection for one another, it did seem out of place for one member to throw another off the balcony.

The well-publicized televangelist scandals of the late eighties did minimal harm to the reputation of the church in our culture—that is, in comparison to the true scandal of our time. The true scandal is the way Christians mistreat one another, fighting and conducting uncivil wars against one another in churches across our nation.

What makes such behavior so scandalous is the special claims we make about our relationships to one another as believers. As Paul says, "Now about brotherly love we do not need to write to you, for you yourselves have been taught by God to love each other" (1 Thess. 4:9).

We claim something that no other religion in the world claims—that God himself makes his home in our lives. That's why ugly and nasty infighting reflects not only on ourselves, but on the character of God. It is no small thing to drag God's character through the mud of acrimony and discord, and at the same time claim he lives within us in all his fullness.

If we had spiritual eyes to see it, whenever we meet another believer we would immediately recognize Jesus living inside each of us. The apostle Paul calls this indwelling Presence a profound mystery, "Christ in you, the hope of glory" (Col. 1:27).

Now if it is the same God, the same Jesus, and the same Holy Spirit living in each of us as believers, how dare we do awful and mean-spirited things to one another and say, "It's what the Lord wanted me to do."

The bank officer looked across his desk in astonishment. The district superintendent and the finance chairman of a Nebraska church were there to request all their bank statements from the last three years. An angry pastor had destroyed all the church's computer and printed financial records when he left. The bank officer was gracious, but seemed shocked as he directed an assistant to begin a microfilm search for all the missing records. It was an embarrassing moment not only for the superintendent and lay leader, but for the cause of Christ as well.

That's why church disharmony damages the credibility of the gospel in the eyes of outsiders. They expect Christians to act differently. When we don't, they wonder if anything about our faith is genuine.

Jesus knew that the church would be believable only if it was loving, compassionate, and of one heart. That's why he prayed for unity on the last night of his life.

When other groups fight, no one gets too unsettled. We expect labor and management to go at it. We know the environmentalists and the oil companies will do battle. And when politicians get down and dirty, its par for the course.

Take the case of a national political convention several years ago. A prominent senator had just lost his bid to become the party's nominee for president of the United States.

The senator who lost was sore. Real sore. Now it's traditional at political conventions for losing candidates to come up on stage and congratulate the victor. It's customary for the two opponents to join hands and raise their arms in a show of unity and reconciliation.

So as the delegates cheered and the balloons rained down, the senator showed up on stage. But he made no move toward the president. So the president graciously walked over to him to extend his hand. But the senator just turned and walked away. The president, perhaps thinking the senator hadn't seen him, walked over to him and again extended his hand. But the defeated candidate snubbed the president and instead waved to someone in the audience.

The incident took place before tens of millions of viewers. The entire nation watched the president of the United States chase the senator around the stage. If you hadn't known it was a political convention, you might have thought you tuned in a ballet. The two never did shake hands. The incident proved to be a "Swan Song" for both men's presidential aspirations.

When a camera crew caught up with the senator outside the building, he flashed a victory sign to the reporters, then climbed into his limousine and sped away. But what victory had he achieved? He had humiliated his opponent and shown a disturbing lack of grace, but was that a triumph? His five-minute display of open animosity and schism made it difficult for those who watched to believe this party was prepared to unite and lead the nation for the next four years.

Much the same impression is left when disunity and discord fill the pews of a local church. When unresolved grievances, wounded pride, and an unforgiving heart are exposed to the outside world, we lose our credibility.

Pastor Thielsen was shaking hands one morning after a worship service when a newcomer introduced himself.

"I just had to come and meet you this morning, Pastor," he said.

Pastor Thielsen was somewhat flattered by his remark.

"Yes sirree," the visitor smiled, "One of your members works at my office. I just had to come and meet the man he can't say anything good about." It's a tragedy when a church becomes more a curiosity than a cause for credibility in a community.

Because unity and harmony validate our faith to the outside world, it's little wonder that our Adversary works so hard to divide the local church into various factions, alliances, and power blocks. If the results weren't so tragic, they might be humorous. I saw a cartoon of a parishioner who was visiting his ailing pastor in the hospital. Shaking his minister's hand, he said, "Good news pastor, the board has decided to send you a get well card. The vote was five to four." Unfortunately, conflict is rarely a laughing matter.

Just about everything you can imagine has been done in the name of a *jihad*, a church holy war. Locks on the church doors have been changed at night to keep one group from gaining access to the building. Petitions calling for the pastor's resignation have been handed out by unofficial ushers on a Sunday morning. Ballot boxes have been stuffed with the proxy votes of elderly members recruited from the nursing homes.

"Just what kind of religion is this?" the sincere unbeliever must ask. "These people should be acting differently."

They're right, Christians should not act this way. We serve a God, a Trinity, whose very nature is love, harmony, and unity.

Jesus will never prompt believers to attack one another, share the latest gossip, or write poison pen letters. Nor will the Holy Spirit ever lead people to drive over a parishioner's lawn, to pour asbestos fibers into an opponent's car transmission, or organize a boycott of giving to win a power play (particularly when the pastor's family or missionaries go without as a result).

God is never behind such actions, for Paul says very clearly, "For God is not a God of disorder but of peace" (1 Cor. 14:33).

Where's the Rest of Me?

Kevin will never forget the night he watched his church tear itself in two. Tempers flared, denunciations were hurled back and forth, and voices reached shouting-level decibels. After the clash was over, a man who played a key role in the chaotic events attempted to justify his behavior. "Before I entered the building tonight, an angel of the Lord specifically directed me to go in and denounce the pastor."

Listen to Paul's words: "But God has combined the members of the body and has given greater honor to the parts that lacked it, so that there should be *no division* in the body, but that its parts should have equal concern for each other. If one part suffers, every part suffers with it; if one part is honored, every part rejoices with it" (1 Cor. 12:24-26).

God does not order the hand to tear off the foot. Nor does he direct the foot to disable the knee. He does not lead one person to break the heart or assault the character of another.

While Ronald Reagan was president, it was popular on college campuses to show some of his old B-grade movies. In one rather odd performance, Reagan plays an individual whose legs are amputated by an unscrupulous doctor. When he wakes up from the operation and realizes what's happened, he begins to shout, "Where's the rest of me?"

Though the movie was far-fetched, and the acting far less than an Oscar-winning performance, the question he raised needs to be asked by local churches. When the pews are empty, when several families are missing, when pastors pack their things and leave with a broken heart, we need to ask, "Where's the rest of me?" The body has lost significant members.

What We Lose in Conflict

For some reason, church conflict doesn't seem as "sinful" as other sins. It doesn't receive the same attention and concern that doctrinal or lifestyle problems attract. It's as if we create a hierarchy of sin, and we assign church conflict to one of the lower rungs, not much worse than jaywalking or forgetting to write a thank-you note.

Some groups even boast about their congregational schisms. They claim that's the way they plant new churches. Like a flatworm, you cut it in half and another section regenerates to take its place. It's a church growth technique.

But let's stop and consider what unresolved and unloving church disputes cost the Body of Christ.

1. We lose our impact in the world.

I have never yet seen a church at war with itself that was able to successfully carry on a meaningful ministry to the unchurched.

A few summers ago we loaded down our station wagon for a month-long vacation to the western United States. Pillows bulged out the windows, suitcases were spring-loaded into the back, and every possible space was crammed with items we couldn't fit anywhere else. With the back end of the car weighed down, we looked like an F-15 Strike Eagle prepared for take off (the only thing we lacked was a canopy and air-to-air missiles).

Half way to our destination, in the dead of night, the car

begin to lurch. When I stepped on the accelerator, the engine roared, but we didn't pick up any speed. We lurched along for several hours until we were able to reach my parent's driveway. As we pulled up, smoke and steam poured from underneath the hood.

The next day we found a mechanic who could examine the car. His face said it all. He broke the news as gently as he could, "Folks, it's a goner."

"What's wrong?" I gulped.

"Well sir, to begin with your transmission is shot."

"There's more?"

"Yup. You've lost your compression in the engine too." He rubbed his jaw. "Funny thing, I've never seen these two go at the same time."

"Guess I'm just lucky," I mumbled.

I asked him how much it would cost to repair the car. He gave me an estimate that was approximately equal to buying my own dealership. After having several garages tell me the same thing, we decided to get rid of the car and lease a new one. Right in the middle of our vacation.

On the outside, everything looked fine. The doors opened, the horn still honked, the flashers still blinked. But when you stepped on the accelerator, the vehicle had no power. Its interior strength was gone. Its essential purpose was spent.

The same can happen to a local church. When serious conflict infiltrates a congregation, the church loses its power, strength, and purpose. It can't attract and keep genuine seekers, it can't motivate or encourage its volunteers, it can't even meet its budget.

The power is gone, and so is its usefulness to God's Kingdom.

2. We grieve the heart of the Father.

Because God is Spirit and invisible to human eyes, we can't see his immediate reaction to our unloving, if not hateful, behavior in the church. But the Bible describes it for us.

Listen to what Paul says about the impact of church fights in his magnificent chapter on church unity found in Ephesians 4: "And *do not grieve* the Holy Spirit of God, with whom you were sealed for the day of redemption. Get rid of all bitterness, rage and anger, brawling and slander, along with every form of malice. Be kind and compassionate to one another, forgiving each other, just as in Christ God forgave you" (vv. 30-32, emphasis added).

Do not grieve the Holy Spirit. We usually think that phrase refers to some personal sin that's offensive to God. Adultery. Murder. Blasphemy. But in the context of Ephesians 4, it's talking about grieving the heart of God when we slander and brawl with one another.

Unfortunately, some people see grieving the heart of God as a small price to pay in order to get their way in a church fight. I have seen grown men and women cry in congregational meetings as they pleaded for unity. Their tears did little or nothing to change the nasty tenor of the meeting. But some day, all of us will have to look directly into the face of a holy God and account for our actions. If our behavior in the local church has caused sorrow, division, and disunity, I suspect one look into his eyes and it will no longer seem such a small matter.

3. *We make it nearly impossible for our children to love the local church or God.*

If I wanted to raise my children to be atheists, I wouldn't remove all copies of the Bible from our home. Nor would I sit them down night after night and lecture them on the nonexistence of God. I wouldn't even spend my time trying to have the motto, "In God We Trust," removed from our coins.

No, I would turn them into little atheists in a much more efficient fashion. I would just let them observe me consistently criticizing the pastor or another church member, refusing to go along with any board or committee decisions, and engaging in vicious gossip about the church leadership. Perhaps for good measure I would also hold a meeting of "concerned members" in my home to discuss the faults and sins of people in the church. Two or three years of such unloving behavior and I could almost guarantee my children would never darken the doors of a church as adults.

Joel grew up in a home where his parents alternated between adoring and despising their pastor. Either he was a saint, elevated to the status of the apostle Peter, or he was a villain on a par with Attila the Hun. Their mood swings continued all through Joel's formative years.

By the time Joel was a young adult, he decided he had enough conflict in his life and didn't need more of it at church. He had been raised to believe pastors were unkind, unreliable, and often evil people. He had been taught that other Christians were selfish and manipulative. Though his parents professed to be Christians, their relentless criticism of those in the church took its quiet toll on his spiritual life.

When Joel married and had children of his own, he chose to raise them outside the church. Why should he put them through the pain he had endured as a child?

Thankfully, God was able to change Joel's heart. Through meeting loving and positive Christians, he was able to trust Christ. He came back to the local church, years later, but only cautiously, tentatively, and with a trunk load of negative memories to unload.

Should we make it that difficult for our children to come to faith in Christ and bond with a body of believers? Most parents would never consciously put roadblocks to faith in their children's way. Yet every time adults roast the pastor, youth pastor, or church member over Sunday dinner, indulge in mean-spirited criticism or hearsay, or give aid or sympathy to divisive people in the church, they are putting large, concrete barricades in front of their children's spiritual journey.

When parents start to criticize Pastor Smith in front of their young children, they might as well substitute the name God for Pastor Smith. In the eyes of young and impressionable children, they are equated as the same thing.

It's an even worse tragedy when parents enlist their children's support in a crusade against the pastor or another group at church. Out of loyalty to their parents, the youngsters will turn all their anger and emotions against the person or persons Mom and Dad are so angry at. Even if the dispute is eventually resolved to the parents' satisfaction, as far as the children are concerned the mean pastor or the mean deacons will always be the mean pastor or the mean deacons.

When parents force their teenagers to leave their youth group because of a church dispute, they are often making a serious mistake. They are forcing their kids to turn their back on the one peer group that has the most potential to have a positive influence on their lives. Is it really best for them to give up their friends, their youth pastor, and run the risk of never joining another group of young Christians, just to make a point?

In the final days of the disintegrating Soviet Union, the government allowed some churches to reopen. Mobs of people flocked back to the church. But the guards posted outside the buildings were given specific instructions: no one under eighteen was to be allowed into the churches. The reasons were obvious. Adults had already made up their minds about God, but young people and children could still be molded and influenced. In this case, the government wanted to raise a generation of atheists.

We in the West rightly denounced such behavior. But when parents belittle and despise their pastor and church leaders at home, they are blocking their children's commitment to the local church just as much as the cynical Soviet officials.

It's a good idea for us to remember the words of Jesus, who warned adults about the consequences of putting spiritual obstacles in the way of our children, "It would be better for him to be thrown into the sea with a millstone tied around his neck than for him to cause one of these little ones to sin. So watch yourselves" (Luke 17:2-3).

4. We give a portion of our lives over to the influence of evil.

Pastor Dickenson had been at his church less than four years when a determined and vocal group of critics began to look for reasons to have him dismissed. One night, an opponent gained access to his office and rummaged through all his personal correspondence. He removed or made copies of any letters he felt would incriminate him.

Next, the group contacted churches where he had previously served. They made a number of long-distance calls to find evidence of wrongdoing in his past. Eventually, they were able to locate someone who had publicly opposed Pastor Dickenson at a previous church.

One morning Pastor Dickenson opened his mail to find an anonymous letter addressed to him. It simply read, "We've talked to Randolph. We have the facts on you." It was signed with a happy face turned upside down.

Breaking and entering, attempting to dredge up dirt from the past, anonymous hate mail—I don't know how these tactics strike you, but they all suggest to me that the influence of evil had somehow taken over a portion of these critics' lives.

The apostle Paul would likely agree. He warned the church in Ephesus, " 'In your anger do not sin': Do not let the sun go down while you are still angry, and do not give the devil a foothold" (Eph. 4:26-27).

Just because two individuals in a church argue with one another does not imply the devil has gained a foothold in either person's life. Not all conflict is the result of evil at work. Some arguments never involve rage or anger, they are simply differing points of view or convictions.

When conflict is treated in a healthy and productive fashion, it can be used to strengthen relationships, improve communication, and clarify goals. But when conflict escalates from problem-solving to the elimination of another person from the group, it has moved from a relatively harmless exercise into the red zone.

One pastor described to me a period of intense confrontation and discontent he endured in his congregation. On four separate occasions he came out to his car and found that his tires had been slashed. The person who sliced the tires did a careful job, causing them to leak slowly and thus go undetected at first. This heightened the chances they would go flat or blow-out on a road far away from home or the church. Evil had gotten a foothold in that person's life. Not only was he guilty of vandalism, he also endangered the life and safety of the pastor and his family.

Violence and threats of violence against one another fall into the same category. A woman told me of a previous pastor who went to any lengths necessary to get his way with the church board. He kept a pistol in his desk drawer. On one occasion, during a serious confrontation in a board meeting, he pulled out the weapon and said, "Let's go outside and settle this thing right now." If memory serves me correctly, she told me the vote went his way.

Not every foothold of the devil in the local church is so obvious. Some evidences are far more subtle, such as lingering resentment, the loss of interest in prayer or reading Scripture, and the desire for revenge.

I recently read of a pastor who went to his supervisor to ask a favor. "Please move me," the pastor said, "My chief opponent in the church is dying of cancer. I don't want to go through the dying process with that s.o.b."

It might shock some people to learn pastors can reach that level of bitterness. But given enough unresolved anger, hurt, and rage, it's possible for any of us to get to the point of turning our backs even on a dying man or woman.

THREE-PART HARMONY

When I was in junior high band, I was convinced I had the gifts of a conductor. When our patient and long-suffering teacher asked for volunteers to direct seventh-grade band, my hand shot up.

He appeared skeptical, but graciously handed over the baton to me and sat down to listen. I looked down at the musical score in front of me. It looked like ancient Sanskrit. I had no idea what I was doing.

So I just raised the baton and counted the way he did, "One and two and three and four and..." The band began to play. We stayed together for two or three measures, then disintegrated into a sound that resembled a truck filled with wild geese and Freon horns colliding with an ambulance.

My teacher was shaken. He had no idea one person could create that much mind-altering noise in such a short time. The chaos and disunity were too painful to listen to. He asked for the baton back and took several moments to regain his composure.

The same is true of the local church. The sound of disunity and discord is painful to our Father's ears. He is a God of unity and harmony. His desire is for the local church to reflect the peace and oneness that characterizes the Trinity. And when he is given the right to conduct the affairs of the church, there is beauty and harmony.

What is unity as the Scriptures define it? It's a spiritual one-ness among believers based on a common desire to obey Jesus Christ and love one another.

Jesus was quite specific about the way we as his followers are to live and relate to each other. Just hours before his arrest and suffering, he prayed for us as future members of the Body of Christ: "I pray also for those who will believe in me through their message, that all of them may be one, Father, just as you are in me and I am in you.... May they be brought to complete unity to let the world know that you sent me and have loved them even as you have loved me" (John 17:20-21; 23).

Jesus prayed that we would be brought to complete unity, a singularity of heart and mind that reflects the loving and harmonious relationship of the Father and the Son. It is as unnatural for believers to be at war with one another in the local church as it would be for the Father and Son to be locked in conflict with one another.

The Father, Son, and Holy Spirit don't argue with one another. They don't engage in power plays with each other, nor do they say nasty things about each other behind the other's back. That's why I find it hard to believe people who create unloving and ugly dissension in the Body of Christ and say, "God told me to do this." God isn't in the business of warring against himself. Jesus said, "A house divided against itself will not stand." That "house" includes the local church.

In one school, an argument erupted between believers over the doctrine of perfection in love. Before it was over, several people were not speaking to each other. The one thing conspicuously absent during much of the debate was love. It reminds me of the Rose Bowl parade the year the Amoco float ran out of gas. It lacked the one resource it was in business to supply to others.

It's not always wrong to disagree with one another, nor is it God's desire that we achieve unanimity in all matters. We are individuals and we will act like individuals. A diversity of opinions can be healthy since no one of us has a complete apprehension of all truth. We all still "see through a glass darkly," as Paul said.

But it is possible to face our differences and still be of one mind—to share a common desire to obey Christ and love one another.

Jesus' express desire for the local church is as clear as pristine waters in a mountain lake: "May they be brought to complete unity to let the world know that you sent me and have loved them even as you have loved me."

The church of Jesus Christ is in need of a Love Storm, a fresh breeze of the Spirit that would unleash harmony in the local church. I'm not speaking of churches uniting under one ecclesiastical banner or mega-denomination. I'm not encouraging the blurring of denominational boundaries or the surrender of certain doctrines to achieve a superficial organizational oneness.

I am referring to a new spirit of unity within each local church that would reflect the beauty and harmony of the relationships that exist in the Trinity.

Jesus said that the way to convince the world he was indeed the Son of God and his love was for real, was for the church to live in harmony and unity.

Imagine, it's not the sophisticated apologetics of Bible scholars, nor the well-orchestrated campaigns of church and parachurch organizations to evangelize a city, nor even the articulate and powerful preaching of well-known expositors that makes Christianity believable. It's Christians getting along with each other.

Paul's prayer for the Colossians has a ring of timeliness for the modern church, "Therefore, as God's chosen people, holy and dearly loved, clothe yourselves with compassion, kindness, humility, gentleness and patience. Bear with each other and forgive whatever grievances you may have against one another. Forgive as the Lord forgave you. And over all these virtues put on love, which binds them all together in perfect unity" (Col. 3:12-14).

The Magnetism of Love

There's something attractive, magnetic, even irresistible about watching love in action, particularly when others attack someone who responds with grace. Marshall Shelley and Kevin Miller tell the story of a pastor they met who had lived through a difficult time of conflict and division in the church.

Brian Wells (not his real name) had led a young man named Larry to faith in Christ just before the trouble broke out. Though the pastor endured months of unfair accusations, anonymous leaflets passed out in the church, and betrayal by members of his own staff, he chose not to retaliate. On one occasion, when he was tempted to preach a scorching sermon aimed at his critics, an older pastor advised him not to do it.

"Truth will win out," the older man assured him.

Larry was a neighbor to one of the men trying to get rid of Pastor Wells. He got a ringside seat to watch the whole ugly event unfold. Finally, he made an appointment to see the pastor. Miller tells what happened next:

> "Pastor," Larry said, "this last year has been awful for me."

> "That sounds rough. Tell me about it," Brian said mechanically.

> "My boss is the most abrasive person I've ever known," he said. "He never has a kind word about anyone or anything. For three years I've sweated under that, and then I came to Community Church—"

> *And you found we Christians aren't any better,* Brian mentally completed his sentence.

> "And I watched you," Larry went on. "I watched the slander, the accusations, all the guff. You had every right to retaliate. And you didn't."

Brian was silent.

"I figured if God could help you not to retaliate, with all you went through, then he could help me not to retaliate with what I went though. So I went back to my boss, and I did something I've never done before in my life—it had to be God, because I couldn't do it—I apologized to my boss, and I asked his forgiveness for the way I bucked him and for the bad attitudes I've had."

Brian opened his mouth to say something, but he couldn't get anything out.

"So that's why I came in here today. I wanted you to know that in the last year you not only helped me meet the Lord, you also proved to me that, in the middle of hard times, God is real."[1]

What had kept Larry from becoming a cynic and turning his back on the local church and Christianity? Brian's attitude and love and patience. Love had gone into action.

What Brian Wells did in the face of criticism and personal attacks is exactly what the apostle Paul suggested we all do when faced with similar situations in the church, "And the Lord's servant must not quarrel; instead, he must be kind to everyone, able to teach, not resentful. Those who oppose him he must gently instruct, in the hope that God will grant them repentance leading them to a knowledge of the truth, and that they will come to their senses and escape from the trap of the devil, who has taken them captive to do his will" (2 Tim. 2:24-26).

Gentleness and kindness may hardly seem like a winning strategy in the face of an all-out assault by an opponent. But to the outside world that watches carefully when Christians argue, such a response is the ultimate proof we are for real. It is proof that the family of God knows and honors the Father's will for unity and harmony, even when push comes to shove.

A Ton of Unity

Just as one individual who allows love to be put into action can have a magnetic pull on others, so an entire church that practices forgiveness and compassion can draw in outsiders.

I had just arrived as pastor at an inner-city church when I received a phone call from a farmer from the central part of the state.

"Pastor, I have got a load of potatoes I'd like to donate to your church if you could use them," he said.

"Sure, why don't you bring them down," I said. I knew several families in the area ran short on groceries each month. This would be an ideal opportunity to demonstrate to the community our concern for them in a tangible way. I was so enthused about the gift I had forgotten to ask him just how many potatoes he was bringing

A few days later I stood astonished as a truck pulled into my driveway and dumped an enormous pile of potatoes into our garage. I suddenly found myself, in the heat and humidity of August, with over a ton of potatoes and nowhere to go. In just a matter of days a smelly liquid began oozing out from underneath the garage door. As far as I know, I was the only pastor in our denomination making vodka in his garage.

I knew something had to be done, so I called a few brave souls from the church and explained my predicament. The next morning about half a dozen of us met and wheeled the rotting potatoes in wheelbarrows down the alley to our church. We spread them out, took a hose to them, then got down on our hands and knees and sorted the over-ripe spuds from the fresh ones.

Curious neighbors stopped to watch grown men and women in the heat of the summer sun sorting through rotting potatoes, one by one. As we began passing out bags of the good potatoes, one baffled woman asked, "Just what type of church is this?"

That event marked the beginning of the church's turn-around after years of decline. As the church united around a common vision of sharing food, friendship, and the gospel of Jesus Christ with our neighbors, an old inner-city church took on new life. Neighborhood residents began visiting the church, and word spread, "This is a church that cares."

People in this world are yearning, if not desperate, to find a group where love and compassion prevail. They're tired of situations where relatives don't speak to each other, business associates stab each other in the back, and political parties play dirty tricks on each other. They're looking for a place where human nature doesn't prevail in all its hostility, malice, and hate.

If the church doesn't offer that alternative, who will?

THE CAUSES OF CONFUSION

If unity and harmony is such a powerful influence in bringing individuals to faith in Jesus Christ, why is it in such short supply in so many churches today? Why do congregations break-up and divorce one another as often as they do? Why are so many pastors sent packing when they would have preferred to stay?

The causes are perhaps as individual as the local church itself. Yet, there are some common patterns in church division that seem to transcend denominational and doctrinal boundaries.

The Loss of Cultural Authority

One contributing factor to the lack of harmony in churches today is the loss of respect for authority. There seems to be no overarching, transcending standard left to regulate human behavior in our society. People have turned away from the government, the courts, and the church to help order their lives. To many, the Ten Commandments is nothing more than the title of a 1950s movie classic starring Charlton Heston and Yuel Brenner.

No one is exempt from this devaluation of respect. Doctors, lawyers, law enforcement officers, and even presidents have lost the respect they once enjoyed a generation ago. Only one out of three Americans now says he trusts the federal government, half the number who had faith in the government twenty years ago.

Add pastors to the list of "endangered authority species." Gone are the days in which the pastor was accorded a position of status in our society. Today, in many quarters, the minister is viewed as nothing more than an employee, a clerical hired hand who is expected to report to a hundred, if not five hundred supervisors.

Some of the sad results of this declining regard for the office of pastor are contained in a 1991 survey of clergy done by the Fuller Institute of Church Growth in southern California:

> Eighty percent [of pastors] believe pastoral ministry has affected their families negatively, 33 percent say being in the ministry is an outright hazard to their family.

> Seventy-five percent report a significant stress-related crisis at least once in their ministry.

> Ninety percent feel they were inadequately trained to cope with ministry demands.

> Fifty percent feel unable to meet the needs of the job.

> Seventy percent say they have a lower self-image now than when they started.

> Forty percent report a serious conflict with a parishioner at least once a month.

> Thirty-seven percent confess having been involved in inappropriate sexual behavior with someone in the church.

> Seventy percent do not have someone they consider a close friend.[2]

If nothing else, these statistics reveal that the job of being a pastor today is not only difficult, it's downright hazardous. A certain portion of these negative conditions has been created by the decline of proper respect and authority.

While pastors have no right to become tin-horn dictators or to abuse their office, Scripture does remind us to show "double honor" to those who preach and teach the Word of God (1 Tim. 5:17). If we can't respect the person, we are at least to respect the office.

The number of forced exits of pastors in one major denomination has jumped from 1 percent annually to over 3 percent. The trend toward forced dismissals of pastors is fueled in part by the cultural influence of a society that has decided to be a law unto itself. We cast aside authority whenever it displeases us or limits our options, even in the church.

This lack of respect for authority affects not only pastors, but also church leaders in general, including elders, deacons, and board members.

"You're not true elders, so I don't have to listen to you," an angry parishioner told an elected board member. The person had decided to reject the board's authority.

When an elder tried to gently reprove a church member by mentioning Scripture, the person responded, "Don't tell me what the Bible says!" Alongside being a pastor, one of the most difficult jobs on earth today is to be a lay leader of a congregation and fight the battle for legitimate respect and authority.

The Cracking of a Vital Pillar

Besides the decline of respect for authority, a second trend at work today is the disintegration of the family. Because healthy families are one of the mainstays of a healthy church, when families get sick, the church soon starts showing ailing symptoms as well.

We were eating breakfast one morning when our sixteen-month-old daughter stood up and dived head first out of her highchair. She immediately vomited.

Fearing she had suffered a concussion, I loaded her, our four-year-old son, and my wife into the front seat of our car. I squealed out of the driveway and headed for the emergency room.

On the way, my daughter got nauseated again.

"Dad?" said my young son.

"What is it?" I said, fingers gripped to the steering wheel.

"The smell is bothering me. I think I'm going to be sick too." Before I could say, "Roll down the window" he threw up in the front seat. I now had two sick children vomiting in the car.

Less than two minutes later my wife, who was pregnant with our third child, said, "Bob?"

"Yes," I replied.

"The smell is getting to me too. I think I'm going to..."

It's amazing how sickness can be passed among family members, isn't it? That's what's happening in the local church today. The divorce rate is nearly identical for church members and for the culture at large. So is the rate for alcoholism, child abuse, and a host of other compulsive, addictive behaviors. Is it any wonder that as families suffer, the church itself is becoming more and more distressed?

Pastor McDermott had just arrived at his new church in New York. On the surface things appeared calm, but it wasn't long until he noticed problems. The church was unable to attract and keep visitors. Finances were on a continual roller-coaster ride. Small brush fires were always breaking out in various ministries of the church.

Soon several in the church started to question if Pastor McDermott was the right man for the job. As the trouble escalated, he began to learn more and more about the personal lives of several people in the church leadership. One key committee leader was a well-disguised alcoholic. Another was secretly seeing the wife of another board member. Yet another was facing criminal charges for illegal gambling practices. When Pastor McDermott attempted to confront these problems, he became the focus of their anger.

In unhealthy families it's the person who points out the problem who is identified as the problem. It's a classic form of group denial. Pastor McDermott discovered that the same rules that apply to a troubled family (don't talk, don't trust, don't feel), also applied to his church. When he tried to address problems, he became the focus of vicious personal attacks. He was allowed to discuss anything he wished, as long as it wasn't the truth.

But just as unhealthy families can produce unhealthy church members, they also produce unhealthy pastors. Clergy from troubled families often become unpleasable perfectionists, unable to give and receive unconditional love and addicted to the approval of others.

Pastor Fred was just such a person. He was raised in a home where love was withheld and his best was never good enough. So Fred grew up with a toxic mix of anger and spiritual shame. When he entered the ministry, he did it to prove to God and others that he was a worthy person. At first it seemed a good fit. The local church offered him the affirmation and approval he craved. But he soon discovered enough was never enough. His unmet needs were still driving his life.

Because of his insecurities, he began to criticize his staff, the leadership, and the church. He approached every board meeting as a win/lose confrontation. His fearful and shame-driven personality soon drove him to find comfort in the attention of other women in the church. While he stayed just on this side of moral impropriety, he engaged in what could properly be termed "emotional adultery."

His unhealthy behavior led to a church filled with anger, suspicion, and discord. It was a great tragedy. Had he been secure in his identity in Christ, his worthiness as a person, and his ability to give and receive love, the atmosphere in the church might have been so much different.

The Unseen Battle

The final prevailing reason for so much dissension and trouble in churches today is one the apostle Paul warned us about nearly twenty centuries ago—spiritual warfare. Listen to his caution to believers: "For our struggle is not against flesh and blood, but against the rulers, against the authorities, against the powers of this dark world and against the spiritual forces of evil in the heavenly realms" (Eph. 6:12).

As a pastor, I could almost predict the appearance of trouble in my church according to how much progress we were making spiritually. If we were gaining successful inroads with neighbors, families, and children, then it was only a matter of time until something would come along to threaten the church's unity. It led me to formulate a spiritual law of Newtonian physics: "For every positive advance, there is an equal and opposite reaction to oppose it."

A pastor arrived at his church one morning to find that the sanctuary had been desecrated. Spiritual warfare is usually not that overt. It more often takes the shape of ugly board meetings, divided factions in the congregation, and severe in-fighting among the staff.

One pastor, serving in the remote regions of Canada, walked out of a painful and acrimonious board meeting and encountered a group of coyotes. They were yelping and howling at him from across the river. "It was as if the devil himself was laughing at us," he sadly observed.

He may have been. For certainly nothing delights our Adversary as much as division and discord in the church. Satan would rather we blame each other than recognize his activity behind the arguments, controversies, and dissensions that split churches and drive believers apart.

Thankfully, there's a remedy to that. Paul says, "Therefore put on the full armor of God, so that when the day of evil comes, you may be able to stand your ground, and after you have done everything, to stand" (Eph. 6:13). We must fight spiritual wars with spiritual weapons, such as fasting and prayer.

When church members pray for one another, forgive one another, and most important of all, love one another, Satan has little or no opportunity to work his stratagems. While he can still roar, he has been effectively de-fanged.

The time has come for a Love Storm to sweep through the local church that reflects the character of God. It's not only possible, it's the Father's will for us.

UNLEASHING A LOVE STORM

The psalmist writes, "How good and pleasant it is when brothers live together in unity!... It is as if the dew of Hermon were falling on Mount Zion" (Ps. 133:1,3). Unity and harmony are refreshing, a sweet scent of mountain air, an exhilarating experience. It ought to be the air we breathe.

I had the opportunity to experience a deep breath of such sweet exhilaration on a most unlikely day—the Sunday after the beginning of Desert Storm. It was a bright and cold January day in Chicago. Just three days earlier the United States and its allies had launched a full-scale attack on Iraq to drive Saddam Hussein's army from occupied Kuwait.

The mood in the congregation was somber and tense. Six young men from the church, including the organist's son, were now on duty in the Persian Gulf. It was the first time I had ever led a church during war time.

What made this situation unique was that at least three

families in this urban church were from Baghdad. They were wonderful people, Armenian Christians, who were now American citizens. They had been in America for at least a decade. They were first generation immigrants whose families had remained behind in the Iraqi capital itself. Several of their cousins and nephews had been conscripted and were now serving in Hussein's army.

I faced a dilemma that Sunday morning. How do you pray for families who have close relatives serving in opposing armies? I turned to a retired minister, a dear friend of mine, for help and advice. As he stood before the congregation, he recalled an experience he had lived through nearly fifty years earlier.

"My friends," he said, "there were nearly 150 men from our church who served overseas during World War II. The women in those days made a banner with the name of each man stitched on it. It hung here in the sanctuary. We prayed, they prayed, we all prayed for their safe return." He paused and looked over the worried faces of the congregation. "I am pleased to say every single man of those 150 returned home safely. I believe God can do the same thing this morning if we pray now as we did then."

Now it was my turn. I invited everyone who had immediate relatives involved in the hostilities to meet with us at the front of the church following the service. The purpose was to pray as the retired pastor had suggested.

Some forty people, men and women, young and old, made their way to the seats near the front of the auditorium following the benediction. The scene at the front of the church was beautiful. Sitting next to each other, elbow to elbow, were families representing many different nationalities, but sharing the same emotions. We all were members of the family of Christ in this local church, and each of us had someone we dearly loved locked in mortal combat thousands of miles away.

For the next sixty minutes or so we brought our concerns to God. I have been in many prayer gatherings in my life, but none that came close to this. It was is if the glory and love of God poured through the ceiling onto our group. The sense of love for one another was overwhelming.

When the meeting ended there was not a dry eye in the group. People found it difficult to say much, but their faces spoke for them. There was joy and serenity in each person's eyes that seemed to say God had already answered our prayers.

Looking back on that memorable Sunday, I now realize what I had experienced. I had been part of a Love Storm, an unleashing of a special spirit of unity and harmony.

So what happened to the men we prayed for? Within just a few months all of the Americans returned home safely. Several stood later that spring in the pulpit to thank the congregation for their prayers.

And what about the relatives in Iraq? It took several months to learn of their fate. But through letters smuggled out by truck drivers from Jordan, we learned that all their relatives, including the soldiers, were safe. Considering the high number of casualties Hussein's army suffered, and the heavy bombing of Baghdad, it was miraculous no one had been killed.

Conclusion

There are many ways to break the heart of a Father, but hatred, antagonism, and discord among his children is one certain way to pierce him with grief. God's will for the local church is for us to act out our love for one another as members of the same family. It's the only way we'll be believable and impact our world.

If Christ's return is delayed, what will future generations say about the family of God as the twentieth century comes to a close and the new millennium begins? What will they find when they sift through the ashes and remains of a local church? Will the records validate our claim that we were brothers and sisters in Christ, or will they tell a different story?

Notes

1. Edward G. Dobson, Speed B. Leas, and Marshall Shelley, *Mastering Conflict and Controversy* (Portland, Ore.: Multnomah Press, 1992).

2. Rolf Zettersten, "Pray for Your Pastor," *Focus on the Family Magazine*, January 1993, 14.

CHAPTER 3

The Dig

THE TIME: A.D. 2295
THE PLACE: THE UNIVERSITY OF
CALIFORNIA AT BERKELEY

G ood morning class," said Dr. Sandra Kincaid, a tall,
slightly sunburned woman. "If everyone will find their
place, we're about to begin."

The twenty or so students in her advanced archaeology class
broke off their conversations and settled into desks in the small
lecture hall.

"I'm pleased to say the initial computer data for our summer
dig has been entered. I'm prepared to present some preliminary
findings this morning," said the fifty-five year old professor. "As
you know, last summer's significant earthquake in the Riverside
area of Southern California revealed the remains of a large structure from the late twentieth century. Initially it was thought to be
a community center of some type, but further analysis of computer diskette fragments found at the site revealed it was the
remains of a church. The Friendship Community Church. Given
the fact it was one of the structures entirely buried by the massive
quake of 2006, the so-called "Big One" as it was known at the
time, this find represents an intriguing opportunity to study religious life and culture at the end of the 1990s."

"Professor?" asked a student who raised his hand.

"Yes, Simonson. What is it?"

"Were there any human remains found at the site?"

The professor eased into a chair at the front of the class. "No, there were not. The building apparently had been vacant for some time, perhaps two or three years. But we're getting ahead of ourselves."

She turned toward her teaching assistant, "Karen, would you activate the holographic virtual reality display?"

"Certainly, professor," she said. The young student walked over to a computerized control panel on the wall and entered a code. The lights went down in the room and a large, three-dimensional image of light appeared in front of the class. In a moment, the blurred image crystallized into a large mound of cement and steel debris right in front of the students. Though only a light image, it was so realistic it gave everyone the feeling of standing at the site of the dig itself.

The professor stood up and with a small laser light pointed to the large glowing image. "As you can see," she began, "the size of this structure is significant. We traced the foundation line that begins here and followed it all around its perimeter." She pushed a button on a remote control device she held in her hand and the image began to rotate. This allowed the students to see the entire foundation structure.

"Our guess is that the Friendship Community Church was at least thirty thousand square feet in its main auditorium, with another three buildings on the same campus that were perhaps five thousand to nine thousand square feet each."

"Were churches really that large at the end of the twentieth century?" asked a student.

"Yes, Cranston," said Kincaid. "It was common for churches to reach sizes of five, even ten thousand members. The late twentieth century was driven by what religious sociologists at the time referred to as 'the church growth movement.' It emphasized strategies to attract large numbers of nonchurch members, and by and large it was successful."

Kincaid pushed another button and the image changed to an aerial view of the excavation site from nearly a thousand feet. "The Riverside dig revealed large deposits of asphalt, a petroleum mixture commonly used in roads and parking lots at the time. We found deposits all the way from one end of the site to the other. By our best estimations, at least seven thousand automobiles could be parked in this area at one time."

"Amazing," whispered one student. "Why would anyone want to be part of such a huge crowed? What brought them there?"

"Computer records from the village zoning board confirm that this church was given permission to build a lot big enough to accommodate at least that many internal combustion vehicles," said Kincaid. "We don't have much more information than that because most city records were destroyed by 'the Big One.' "

Another student raised her hand.

"Yes, Morris?" the professor said.

"Is it your impression that this church was usually filled to capacity?"

"Definitely. As I said, we were able to recover a limited number of computer records from the site. Mainly 'diskettes,' as they were called back then. They contain the morning worship 'bulletins.' " She flicked the remote control in her hand twice and a large sheet of white paper appeared in front of the class.

"Wow," said someone near the back. "This is like looking at parchments from the Dead Sea Scrolls."

"Perhaps not as ancient as those documents, Johnson," Kincaid said. "But I agree, these are valuable fragments. Let me show you something else intriguing." The text on the image suddenly jumped in size so the letters were at least six inches tall. It read, "We are pleased to announce that the elders have decided to institute a third worship service starting at 8:00 A.M. on Sunday, March 23. The decision has been made in order to ease the crowded conditions at the 9:30 and 11:00 A.M. services."

"Professor, you said earlier the church had been vacant for a number of years before its final destruction in the earthquake. How do you account for that?" asked a student.

"That's the real challenge of the Riverside dig," said Kincaid, a sly smile on her face. "That's where we trade the role of scientist for that of detective. How is it that a building went from holding perhaps as many as fourteen thousand people on Sunday morning, to standing virtually empty for nearly three years? I have a preliminary theory, but let's wait a moment for that.

"By last August we found evidence that the initial structure had been much smaller than the larger buildings that followed. Using a spectra-analysis of the chemical composition of the foundation blocks we found on one side of the site, we date the original building to, say, 1978 or so, the beginning of an era of dramatic church expansion among certain groups."

"So Friendship Church grew rapidly during this time," said a class member.

"Exactly. I speculate that the early years of this church were marked by enthusiastic, aggressive programming and growth. The computer fragments indicate that the church offered a wide variety of programs to members and to the community."

"Such as what?" someone asked.

The professor just smiled and pushed her hand-held device. Suddenly a large orange and blue plastic object appeared in front of the class.

"What in the world is that?" Morris asked.

"It's a piece of a child's toy," Kincaid said. "We discovered it in what we think was the nursery section of the structure. It was most likely a toy slide. Based on numerous other relics we found, we have concluded the church must have run an extensive program for children." Kincaid pushed another button, and a yellow rectangular object appeared. "This is a cafeteria tray, found near the remains of what must have been the kitchen. Based on the size of the room, we believe the church was able to serve meals to large groups. Perhaps they sponsored an adult day-care center or a so-called soup kitchen for needy people in the community."

A large sheet of music appeared next before the class. "This is one of my favorite finds of the summer," said Kincaid. "It's a sheet that was used in group singing. Note carefully the words, 'We are one in the Spirit, we are one in the Lord.' Apparently this group embraced a concept of group unity or cohesion that they frequently emphasized in their music."

The professor smiled, as if she knew something the others in the class did not.

"I still don't get it," said a student sitting in the front row. "Here you have a church with large numbers of children, a program that helps large numbers of people in the community, and has an emphasis on group cohesion. Why did it die out?"

"I can tell you when, much easier than I can tell you why, the church went into decline," Kincaid said. "A search of bulletin records indicates that a drop-off in weekly support began in the final three years of the twentieth century. I've charted this drop-off."

The next image to appear was a three-dimensional bar graph. The large red, blue, and green bars glowed in the darkness of the classroom. The bars were anywhere in size from six feet to two feet high. They illustrated the significant increases in annual giving to Friendship Church beginning in 1978 all the way up until 1998. Then, in each of the years following, the giving started to drop. Slowly at first, then all at once, it seemed to fall off the edge of some precipice.

"By the year 2002, giving was only 30 percent of what it had been a decade earlier," mused Kincaid. "By then, it was apparently too late to reverse the trend." She paused and looked at the bewildered students. The professor got up and stood next to the graph that was as tall as she was. Pointing to it with her laser light, she said, "There it is. The year 1999. The critical year something happened at Friendship Community Church that eventually spelled its doom."

"Does the fall-off in giving correlate to the economic recession that occurred at the end of the decade?" asked Morris, an economics minor.

"No," Kincaid said. "Macroeconomic problems can't explain the demise of Friendship Community Church. Even though unemployment was at a record high in Southern California at the time due to excessive deficit spending, we have reason to believe that giving at other churches in the area actually went up. Religious individuals tend to give more, not less, during periods of economic hardship."

"Was it outside persecution?" asked another student. "My history of religion professor said the turn of the millennium was marked by attacks on the church by militant groups in the society."

"Interesting you should say that," Kincaid said. "Look at this document." A soiled and faded brochure crystallized before the class. "For those of you who can't read that from the back, let me help you." The professor pointed the control at the screen, and the computer erased the dirt and water marks from the page and produced sparkling, bright copy.

"Join us in a March for Life on June 22," it read. "Friendship Community will join thousands of other believers this Sunday in a demonstration of support for the sacredness of human life."

"Abortion was still legal in that decade," said Kincaid. "And churches that objected to the law eventually had their tax-exempt status removed. It was a clear effort to intimidate them into silence."

"I can't believe it was ever legal in the United States," a female student said from the back of the class.

"I can," said an African-American student. "There was a time when slavery was lawful in the United States too."

"It is one of the tragedies of our history we must live with as a nation," said Kincaid. "Friendship Community, according to the archives of the *Los Angeles Times*, was stripped of its tax-exempt status and its pastor arrested for refusing to pay taxes over the abortion issue. But again, that incident correlates with an increase in giving and attendance, not a decrease."

"Of course," said a student. "Persecution actually strengthened the church. It drew them together."

"The blood of the martyrs is the seed of the church, or so the old saying goes," said Kincaid. "Let's go back to 2003, the year before we think the church closed its door. Our content analysis of bulletin fragments reveals an increase in the frequency of calls for volunteers. Numerous programs were beginning to be phased out at this point for lack of staff. The number of employees at the church was also cut in half. We know this by examining the annual budget report we found on one of the diskettes."

"Did you find evidence that the building itself was beginning to deteriorate, professor?"

Kincaid smiled. "I was hoping you would ask that. What do you think these three objects are?"

A holograph image of a woven cloth fragment appeared in the air. Next to it were a variety of small beige chips of some sort. Finally, next to both of these objects was a gold, silk-like piece of material with holes in it.

"Who would like to be our Baker Street sleuth?" asked the professor. She could read a dig with the skill transportation experts could reconstruct a crash site.

"The first object is a piece of carpet," ventured one student. "Those appear to be strands of Dacron."

"Very good," said the professor. "Now why is it significant?"

The student rubbed his hand on his chin, then a light went seemed to go on. "Because it's worn-out and thread-bare. It was never replaced. The church didn't have the funds to install new carpet because they were in a financial crisis."

"You really don't need me, do you?" said Kincaid in a good-natured way. "How about the paint chips?"

The young man enjoyed the affirmation he had received in front of his peers, so he pressed on. "Okay, the paint chips. They look just like ordinary paint from that era."

"Well," said Kincaid, "would it help if I told you it was a latex mixture?"

"That's it!" he said. "Latex was used only up until the turn of the century. That's when chemical engineers introduced the genetically engineered Sytax, a paint that would last for a century."

"Go on," said Kincaid.

"It must mean the building was never painted again after the 1990s. A sign that people had lost interest in its upkeep. There were fewer and fewer people attending so less attention was given to the physical structure."

"You're two for three, Mr. Johnson. Now for the silk fragment."

"I'm stuck on that one," he replied.

"I think I know, professor," said a young woman. "In my undergraduate music theory class we learned it was common in the twentieth century for church groups to wear common robes when they sang. That silk looks like a portion of a choir robe."

"And?" said the professor.

"And the holes in it are from insect infestation. Which means the robes must have been stored for an extraordinary period of time. They ended up moth-eaten."

"Congratulations," said the professor. "I have just a few more relics to show you, and then I'll offer my theory on the death of

Friendship Community Church."

The professor punched a code into her hand-held device and two large brass door knobs appeared before the class.

"So what's so unusual about those?" asked a student. "Every building had door locks in that century. It was before laser access security was introduced on a popular level."

"Look more closely," the professor said. "These two locks were found at separate places on the dig site. One was from where we think the front door was, the other from what must have been a side door."

The images rotated and revealed a computer schematic design of the interior of the locks. The class was silent for several seconds as they analyzed the data.

"These are two different locks, which would require two different keys," said one student. "But why would a church have different locks for the same outside doors. Wouldn't that just create confusion and an inconvenience?"

"What if there were two groups who both wished to control access in and out of the building?" the professor asked. "Particularly to keep the other group from entry into their portion of the building?"

"I get it," said one student out loud. "Two groups must have emerged in the final days of the church, each claiming the building belonged to them. They changed locks to keep their opponents out of the building. But wasn't this the same group that stressed unity and cohesion as part of their doctrinal beliefs?"

"We're almost finished," said Kincaid. "This is the last piece of the puzzle. We found it in late September, just before we had to close down the dig for the year."

The professor turned the lights back on and held up a document encapsulated in a vacuum-sealed file. "I particularly prize this find. It's a letter we found in a file cabinet that was buried in rubble. We were able to retrieve most of the documents from this steel cabinet, though moisture and age has caused considerable decay."

She held up the clear file that contained the fragment. "Unfortunately, half the letter is missing. We only have this top fragment. But I believe it gives us the final link in the mysterious demise of Friendship Community Church. Now let me put this up on the image enhancement screen."

The lights went down and a wrinkled, brown piece of stationery, with an official letterhead, appeared before the students. "Let me magnify this for you," said Kincaid. The letter suddenly jumped up twice its size.

"It's written in dot-matrix, a type of computer printing system of the late twentieth century. Allow me to read it to you. It's dated, July 17, 2003." The professor put on a pair of half-glasses and began to read.

"*Dear Reverend Baxter, I have concluded my meetings with the different factions in your church. I have tried to be fair and hear all sides objectively. Mr. Swanson, who speaks for the aggrieved members of his group, insists that nothing less than your resignation will restore peace to the church. He has indicated that he will publicly call for a vote of no confidence at the next quarterly business meeting.*

"*I met next with Mr. Delaney, to try and determine the nature of his hostility toward you. He accuses you of biblical heresy, unethical financial conduct, and abuse of your office. He has filed charges with the denominational office and indicates he will continue to press for a significant financial boycott until you are removed.*

"*I was able to meet with his wife, Mrs. Susan Delaney, who shared information more helpful to me. She indicated that her husband's displeasure and anger with you dates back to a church banquet four years ago. He arrived that night under the impression that he was to be a guest at the head table. But when he attempted to sit down next to you, you informed him that the place was reserved for someone else.*

"*I have asked the leaders of this faction to meet with us to arbitrate this dispute, but they refuse. He also refuses to participate in any service of reconciliation with you. Unless this matter is dealt with, Reverend Baxter, I fear..."*

That's where the letter ended.

The class sat speechless.

"You mean a church of over ten thousand people was destroyed over an argument about who would sit at the head table?" someone said.

"I'm afraid so," Professor Baxter said. "Would someone please turn on the lights?"

CHAPTER 4

How to Split
Your Church

How is it that a thriving and growing church can be split in half? The reasons may be as profound as doctrinal deviations and as insignificant as who sat where at a church banquet. But the result is the same: the family of God is divided and a chain reaction of events is set in motion that proves enormously destructive, sometimes cataclysmic.

Now that the Cold War is essentially over, a number of fascinating stories and documents have been released that detail the efforts of the old Soviet Union to infiltrate the most closely guarded secret of this century: the development of the atom bomb in the desert of New Mexico during World War II. A former top Soviet spy master's memoirs contain startling information on how they were able to accomplish that intelligence coup.

The Russian's most disturbing revelation is that Robert Oppenheimer, sometimes known as the father of the atomic bomb, passed along to the Stalin government vital secrets about splitting the atom. This and other such information contributed to the Russians' successful explosion of their own nuclear device in 1949. That event set the stage for a tense, sometimes terrifying, forty-year nuclear stand-off between the United States and the Soviet Union.

In the spirit of declassifying such closely guarded secrets, I'd like to reveal the ten essential steps to splitting not an atom, but a local church. Each of these steps, if followed carefully and with precision, will unleash a chain reaction that will vaporize the unity and harmony of the local church in a mushroom cloud of discord and bitterness. The fallout will continue for years.

Step One: Focus exclusively on your own desires.

This may seem a relatively harmless or minor first step to take to divide an entire church, but don't despise the day of small things.

A church in the southern United States no longer exists, due in part to a scene that took place in the church kitchen one Sunday afternoon several years ago.

A new family had recently joined the congregation. They arrived with enthusiasm to take part in their first pot-luck luncheon. The aroma of tuna casseroles, baked beans, and tater-tot dishes wafted through the building.

"Why don't you go find us a place to sit," said the wife to her husband. "I need to drop off my salad in the kitchen."

Now most observes would guess the church sanctuary is the modern day equivalent of the holy of holies found in the tabernacle of Old Testament times.

Wrong.

In many churches, it is the kitchen, though the nursery now seems destined to replace it. At least in my parent's generation, there were unwritten rules and procedures that governed the activities and culture of the church kitchen. Some were far more complicated, ritualistic, and severe in their punishments than anything the Pharisees ever cooked up.

This day the unsuspecting newcomer cheerfully entered the kitchen and dropped off her red gelatin salad. She then headed back to the main fellowship hall to take her place next to her family.

She sat down just as the pastor bowed his head and asked the blessing on the event. The moment he said 'Amen,' hungry parishioners politely charged for the serving line. There were dozens of dishes to scrutinize, sample, and scoop.

"Where's our salad?" the woman's husband asked innocently.

"It should be right here with the others," she replied. Her eyes scanned the salad table from one end to the other. There was a tossed green salad, a bowl of potato salad, a pan of coleslaw, and last, but not least, a durable green salad with sliced carrots in the middle topped off with mayonnaise (a good deal of that still remained).

"I don't see ours anywhere," said the husband.

"There must be some mistake," said the wife. "I'll go find out what happened." She handed her husband her plate and headed toward the kitchen. She arrived at the kitchen door just in time to witness the queen of the kitchen ladling the last of her salad into the garbage disposal.

"What are you doing?" the newcomer shrieked. "That's my salad!"

Without batting an eye, the woman looked up and said, "You're new to this church. You'll soon learn we use only real whipped cream around here, not Cool Whip." She then hit the switch. The garbage disposal rumbled and gurgled, and the salad was sucked down the drain going from this life to the next.

That one incident proved to be the start of a significant church battle that escalated into all-out war.

The book of James contains an explanation of what happened in the kitchen. It's a fundamental principle of church conflict that helps explain why believers can start throwing salad at one another. "What causes fights and quarrels among you? Don't they come from your desires that battle within you? You want something but don't get it" (James 4:1-2).

James says the most elementary, basic, rudimentary way to split a church is to focus exclusively on what you want and then do what you must to get it. Perhaps you prefer praise choruses to hymns, or you like verse-by-verse preaching rather than topical messages, or you believe no church should start building until all the monies are in the bank, rather than allow for reasonable short-term debt. There's nothing wrong with expressing differing view-points on these issues. All of us have a right to our convictions.

The problems begins when we allow our preferences or convictions to become elevated to the level of an absolute. It's when we insist on having things done our way, and our way only, that factions, divisions, and heartache often enter the life of the local church.

Does that mean you or I should go through life without convictions? Of course not. But we need to keep in mind the distinctions between biblical absolutes, group convictions, and personal preferences.

A *biblical absolute* is a clear, unmistakable, foundational truth of Scripture. For example, I don't believe anyone can legitimately call themselves a Christian if they don't believe in the atoning suffering, death, and resurrection of the Lord Jesus Christ. That's an absolute bedrock tenet of our faith.

A *group conviction* usually involves the interpretation of Scripture on matters other than the essentials of orthodox Christianity. Various denominations have appeared as the result of differing views. Group convictions are an important part of our faith, but they are one step beneath the level of biblical absolutes such as the Virgin Birth.

Personal preferences are matters that are more difficult to establish from Scripture. Styles of music, methods of preaching, and various techniques used in evangelism might fall into this category. Again, these are important matters, but less clear from

Scripture than a group conviction or a biblical absolute.

When we confuse the difference between secondary and primary issues of the faith, and when we insist on our desires ruling the day, we can end up tearing apart a local church. The answer is not to surrender all convictions and preferences and to live passive and apathetic lives. It is to agree to live theologically informed lives, search and study the Scriptures, and agree to disagree on matters less than biblical absolutes. In all this, we should strive to maintain the unity of the Spirit in the bond of love. But if splitting the church is our aim, we should insist our viewpoint is the only one permissible when it comes to minor matters. Refuse to listen and attack others with a judgmental heart. It will pay off.

Step Two: Listen to every criticism you hear.

The next step in splitting a local church is to give credence to every rumor, story, or criticism you happen to hear. The morsel of gossip doesn't have to be true to be destructive. That's the genius of gossip—you just have to treat it as true for it to do its ugly work.

On one occasion the word around our church was that I owned expensive, imported furniture. I have no idea how the rumor started, but it soon had gained a life of its own.

Well, the truth was our furniture was imported—from the top floor of J.C. Penney—where all the other close-out items were arranged. But the expensive part baffled me. Perhaps they were adding to the value of the furniture all the overdue library books that had fallen down behind the cushions. In that case, our love seat and sofa belonged in Windsor Castle.

Though it was just a small, silly rumor that eventually died out for lack of truth, it carried a sinister suggestion. It introduced the notion that the pastor was living in the lap of luxury at the expense of struggling parishioners. One trip to our home would have quickly dispelled the notion of opulence. Most of our furnishings were "early seminary."

Solomon, perhaps the wisest ruler to ever live, made this simple observation, "Without wood a fire goes out; without gossip a quarrel dies down" (Prov. 26:20).

Rumors, gossip, baseless criticisms—they all need oxygen and combustible material to catch fire. If you deprive those harmful substances of a listening ear and sympathetic response, they quickly die out. But all too often we listen to things we should not. Someone has juicy news about trouble in the youth pastor's marriage, or a fight that is brewing in a Sunday school class over letting a staff member go, or whispers that a deacon has changed his doctrinal beliefs.

There may or may not be an element of truth to these stories. But the high road of integrity is to go to the persons involved and ask in a straight-forward fashion, "Is this true?" If we're not willing to take that step, we have no business repeating the story.

But if your goal is to split a church, you should do just the opposite. Keep circulating the story without ever verifying its accuracy. The longer the rumor circulates, the more people's emotions become inflamed, the more groups form stubborn opinions, and the more enormous personal hurt can be inflicted on innocent people.

An analogy might be helpful. We have some rather odd electrical wiring in our home. We're not able to run the microwave, toaster, and air conditioner all at the same time. If we do, a little switch goes click and we are instantly transported back into the Dark Ages.

The reason is the circuit breaker in the basement. That device is a simple switch that interrupts the flow of electricity when the system overloads. Though frustrating to us at times, circuit breakers prevent potential fires from overheated wires.

Every church needs circuit breakers. These are the brave individuals who in the middle of hearing a juicy story, turn and say, "Excuse me, Jeff, but have you gone to this person and asked if this is true?" Nine times out of ten, the answer will be no. These people then say, "Would you mind if I go to the person you just named, tell them I heard this story from you, and ask them if it's true?"

I guarantee that you will hear something go click. The rumor will most likely die right then and there. You'll have snipped the overheated wires of gossip and the energy will suddenly stop flowing. And, chances are, you'll never be included again in the circuit of hot gossip.

Solomon said, "The words of a gossip are like choice morsels; they go down to a man's inmost parts" (Prov. 26:22). To split a church, make sure the people in it are fed a steady diet of embarrassing, inappropriate, and distorted information. Then watch the sparks fly.

Step Three: Focus on your pastor's weaknesses, not his strengths.

To seriously disrupt a local church, target for discussion and continual criticism the imperfections and shortcomings of the pastor.

One of my favorite "Far Side" cartoons is two deer bucks standing in the woods having a conversation. A large circular target is painted on the side of one of the deer. The other one says to him, "Bummer of a birthmark, Ralph."

There is a sense in which every pastor carries around a large target painted on his back. He can quickly become the focal point of everything that's wrong with the church. That's not too surprising. Who else besides the pastor and staff so clearly represents the identity, mission, and integrity of the church?

A pastor from the West Coast tells the story of a woman who arranged for an appointment in his office. She brought with her several typed pages of complaints about the way the office was managed. She pointed out spelling errors in the bulletin, dates and times when the phones went unanswered, and blunders staff members had made in making the announcements on Sunday morning.

As she clicked off her seemingly endless list of shortcomings, problems, and mistakes the pastoral staff had made, the pastor became increasingly depressed.

Are there really people out there who make it their life's ambition to keep track of all these things? he thought to himself. The woman stopped her recital of grievances only long enough to look up and make sure he was still listening. As she turned to page four of her indictments, the pastor's eyes glazed over.

The surest way to discourage a pastor is to point out all that he does wrong in a given week. Like the sensation of dull heartburn, a pastor will carry around a heavy sense of emotional indigestion. Over time, if he's not given relief, that heartburn will turn to an ulcer of disillusionment, and finally to the internal hemorrhaging of despair.

Pastor Riddell had always wanted to live by the ocean. The call to this Mid-Atlantic church was a dream come true. He had been there less than a year when the onslaught of criticisms started. First he was faulted for using too much humor in his sermons. "Undignified," "egotistical," "sacrilegious" were the words used to describe his preaching. He adjusted his sermon to a more serious tone, but when he did, a little of the light in his eyes went out.

Soon Pastor Riddell was criticized for not joining the church softball team. He was already tied up several nights of the week attending board and committee meetings, not to mention doing visitation. There simply wasn't enough time in his week. But when he attempted to explain his predicament, his critics charged he was "arrogant" and "too conceited" to associate with people. He gave up trying to defend himself, and a little more of the light went out in his eyes.

Then Jim came to visit him. Jim was a lay person who considered himself a Bible scholar, though he had no formal training.

"Pastor," he said as he leaned back in a chair, "several of us are concerned about your preaching. We don't feel it's biblical."

"What do you mean it's not biblical?" he asked. "Am I misinterpreting something?"

"We just don't feel you're doing your homework," said Jim. "We don't feel we're getting the teaching we need."

Pastor Riddell explained how he worked hard on his messages, often translating each Sunday's text from the original language. But that didn't satisfy Jim.

The next week, as Pastor Riddell stood to preach, he noticed several of his critics had brought laptop computers with them. "They're trying to catch me on something," he thought to himself. As they tapped away during the service, a little more of the remaining light in his eyes went dim.

He was hard at work in his office one day when he received a long-distance phone call.

"Pastor Riddell, is that you?" came a familiar, friendly voice.

"Alan? It's so good to hear from you again," he replied. Alan had been a member of the board at Pastor Riddell's last church. The two had worked closely together for several years and had built an enduring friendship.

"Uh, pastor, I wish I didn't have to tell you this," Alan said. "I received a phone call yesterday from one of the members of your church. They called to see..."

"Yes?"

"They called to see if you had caused trouble here, too."

"They what?" Pastor Riddell said, half-standing, half-sitting at this point.

"I told them we loved you, and that we missed you very much," Alan said. "I just thought you should know."

Pastor Riddell put down the receiver slowly, then sat down again. The remaining little flicker of life and joy, now only a shadow of its former brightness, finally went out.

Within a few weeks, he submitted his resignation to the board, never to return to full-time pastoral ministry. Shortly after his departure, several other families left the church as well.

Pastors are human, which means they are imperfect, frail, and make mistakes. But perfection and infallibility have never been a part of the biblical job description for a shepherd. The writer of the book of Hebrews understood just how difficult a job it is to be a pastor. That's why he wrote to church members, "Obey your leaders and submit to their authority. They keep watch over you as men who must given an account. Obey them so that their work will be a joy, not a burden, for that would be of no advantage to you" (Heb. 13:17).

It is of no advantage to a congregation to continually nit-pick, fault-find, and criticize their pastor. It's no advantage unless—your objective is to divide and demoralize the church. In that case, it accomplishes your goal very effectively.

Step Four: Speak the truth or practice love, but never combine the two.

If I were to try and undermine the spiritual health of a local church in an insidious way, I wouldn't begin by introducing false teachings. The more mature members would quickly spot them and call the congregation back to scriptural teachings.

Instead, I would emphasize truth or love, but never balance the two in my conversations or relationships with others.

Let me illustrate what I mean. Pastor Danielson was by nature a nonconfrontive person. He was what conflict management experts call a "teddy bear." He was so concerned about keeping the peace and offending no one that he rarely, if ever, called anyone to account for their actions. If financial affairs were handled in a slipshod way by volunteers, he said nothing. He didn't want them to quit. If a Sunday school teacher led a questionable life during the week, he said nothing. The church, after all, is where everyone should be accepted for who they are. If staff members didn't do their jobs, he said little. Love, not criticism, is what builds a church, he reasoned.

Over a period of years, problems in the church accumulated like a hallway closet that's never cleaned out. Audits were never done to insure proper handling of money. Parents were never called to investigate their concerns about the behavior of sponsors working with their teenagers. Staff members were allowed to run their own little fiefdoms with little or no accountability.

Because Pastor Danielson wanted to be known as a lover rather than a fighter, he decided to take another church rather than face the backlog of problems.

The pastor who followed him never knew what hit him. The accumulated problems spilled over like soap suds from a washing machine in an old "I Love Lucy" episode.

Reverend Jacobs, on the other hand, thrived on confrontation. He hadn't put in a full day until he called someone on the carpet. His sermons often sounded like forty-minute scoldings. He berated people for their lack of faith, prayer, and service. He said he was preaching truth, but to many people he sounded just plain angry.

If Reverend Danielson was a "teddy bear," conflict management experts would classify Reverend Jacobs a "shark," a competitor who is out to win every contest he enters. He had little time for relationships. He avoided hospital calls because he felt awkward when confronted by people's suffering. He did as little counseling as possible because he found it irritating to listen to people's inner turmoils. As he saw it, he had more important things to do than sit and hold hands.

Ironically, no one felt more betrayed and incensed when the church voted him out than did Pastor Jacobs. He was shocked by how little mercy his congregation showed toward him. What he didn't realize is that he had trained his people to be sharks. It was only logical that someday they would catch his blood scent and circle his life raft.

Churches that stress love, to the exclusion of speaking the truth, will eventually collapse on themselves. The weight of unaddressed problems and conflicts will bring the ceiling down. They will end up with a basement full of upstairs.

On the other hand, churches that pound hard on the truth, but fail to see the value of love and compassion, will eventually devour each other. Robspierre, one of the last men to lose his head to the guillotine during the French Revolution, had used the same device countless times to relieve his enemies of their heads.

If both Pastor Danielson and Pastor Jacobs failed their congregations by their conflict management style, then what's the answer?

The solution is to do what the Scriptures quite plainly tell us to do in our interactions with one another, "Instead, speaking the truth in love, we will in all things grow up into him who is the Head, that is, Christ" (Eph. 4:15).

A grown-up, healthy church is one that knows how to speak truthfully to each another, yet in a loving and gracious spirit.

I remember one summer attempting to plant a garden in my backyard. I had only a small patch next to the house that got sunlight during the day, so I decided to make the most of it. In a space no more than twelve feet by six feet, I planted sugar snap peas, green beans, carrots, tomatoes, bell peppers, and five rows of corn (three kernels per hill). To my delight, everything germinated. The garden exploded in green. Everything shot up.

Within a month, you couldn't see a patch of ground. Within another month, it had turned into a dense jungle, an Amazon rain forest of the Midwest. We would hear strange animal sounds and bird calls in the early morning. One night we were certain we heard Johnny Weismueller in the backyard.

A friend of ours, who is a talented gardener, came over to look at my overgrown plot. I wasn't there at the time. But my wife tells me Linda started to giggle, then laugh, then finally began to cry. Cheryl claims she ultimately had to be helped to her car.

But when she called to discuss my garden on the telephone, she simply said in a gracious and calm voice, "Bob, I think you planted too many things in too small a space." She had spoken the truth in love.

Now if she had only emphasized the truth, she could have said, "Bob, Miracle Grow has a warrant out for your arrest."

Or if she had wanted simply to emphasize love, she could have said, "Bob, it's not what you harvest, it's what you plant that counts."

Either way, if we speak only truth or love, we will lose the balance Scripture directs us to maintain. Ultimately, it will undo the church.

Step Five: Store grievances for future use.

One effective means of crippling the life and vitality of a local church is to encourage people to harbor secret resentments against one another. The longer individuals store these grievances, the more powerful they become.

I read a number of years ago about a strange neurological illness that afflicted a certain community. The odds were too great for all those people to come down with the same symptoms: tingling fingers, loss of energy, and blinding headaches. Health authorities were baffled.

After toxicologists and state health officials interviewed a number of residents, an old-timer remembered that during the Depression, farmers would mix toxic chemicals near that site for use as a pesticide. Sure enough, as the scientists tested the soil at the old site, they found serious concentrations of poison that continued to seep into the ground water.

Buried resentments are a great deal like toxic chemicals. They are often invisible, can go undetected for years, and will eventually create problems that have no apparent cause.

One church fight eventually ended up in a state court. Both sides of the dispute claimed the church property belonged to them, and each had sued the other to gain title to the building and land. The high court refused to rule on the case and instead referred the matter to the denominational court. After a long and lengthy investigation, the cause of the bitter dispute was traced back to a church banquet where one member had received a larger slice of ham than the other.

Whether the story is true or not, buried resentments can do enormous damage. They often go back generations. One church leader believes unresolved bitterness is probably behind his church's penchant for chewing up one pastor after another. Somewhere, sometime, someone had allowed a wrong or injustice to become deeply embedded in their soul. Like toxic chemicals hidden in the soil, it poisoned generations to come.

The writer of Hebrews warns us, "See to it that no one misses the grace of God and that no bitter root grows up to cause trouble and defile many" (Heb. 12:15). Did you notice that last phrase, "and defile many"? The result of storing grievances is the corruption of many people.

Unless past grievances and wrongs are resolved, forgiveness given and received, and true reconciliation effected, the ability of the church to be the church is paralyzed.

But if division and disunity is the objective, buried resentments, like buried toxic waste, are an effective means of disabling future generations of believers.

Step Six: Forgive only those who ask you to do so (and only if they deserve it).

I once challenged a man to forgive another man he had been holding a thirty-year grudge against.

"Why should I forgive him?" he shouted. "He's never admitted he was wrong."

"Because Christ tells us to forgive our enemies," I replied.

"No!" he said trembling with anger. "Christ only forgave the thief on the cross who asked him for forgiveness. I won't forgive him until he asks me to."

The man had invented his own clever theological argument to justify his hatred toward his enemy.

To keep church disunity and disharmony going strong, it's important Christians forgive only those who ask for it, and then, only if the people change.

But the man in this story had misread Scripture, as people who refuse to forgive often do to justify their angry behavior.

In Luke's account of the death of Jesus, the moment after the nails were driven into his hands and feet Jesus cried out, "Father, forgive them, for they do not know what they are doing" (Luke 23:34). Notice, no one had asked for Jesus' forgiveness—not the soldiers, not the bystanders, not even the criminals. He offered pardon not because they begged for it, nor because they deserved it, but simply because they needed it.

Even the thief on the cross never said 'forgive me,' though he confessed his sinfulness, " 'We are punished justly, for we are getting what our deeds deserve. But this man has done nothing wrong.' Then he said, 'Jesus, remember me when you come into your kingdom.' Jesus answered him, 'I tell you the truth, today you will be with me in paradise' " (Luke 23:41-43).

There are two elements to forgiveness. One is the canceling of a moral debt someone owes us; the other is the restoration of the relationship. The two don't always occur at the same time.

You or I may have to wait a lifetime to hear someone who has wronged us say, "I'm sorry. Please forgive me for what I did." We may or may not hear those words in this life. But the Bible makes it uncomfortably clear that we are to forgive others whether or not they ask for it, "Then Peter came to Jesus and asked, 'Lord, how many times shall I forgive my brother when he sins against me? Up to seven times?' Jesus answered, 'I tell you, not seven times, but seventy-seven times' " (Matt. 18:21-22).

There's to be no limit, no precondition, no fine print in our willingness to forgive others. If we forgive others simply because they deserve it, that is justice. But if we forgive others simply because they need it, that's mercy.

Pastor Friedrich was undergoing an annual review by a committee from his church. He asked a simple question that turned out to be spring-loaded. "What could I do to better serve you this next year?" he asked the committee.

He might as well have been a fat rooster pheasant sitting on top of a corn stalk in November asking half a dozen hunters armed with .12 gauge shotguns, "Who'd like to try first?"

Suddenly a man flushed red, and with a quivering voice said, "Pastor, my sister Margaret had gout last February and you never visited her. Not once! Is a simple visit too much to ask?"

Pastor Friedrich was only employed part-time at the church. He was not told of Margaret's condition for three weeks. He in fact had tried to visit her, but unfamiliar with the country roads, he had gotten lost one winter evening trying to find her and nearly ended up in a ditch.

"I apologize, I'm sorry I missed her," he said.

"Hmmph," said the man, his arms crossed and his expression an unrelenting scowl.

That's the type of stubborn unforgiveness that will eventually spread like a cancer through a church. Demanding that others beg for our pardon, requiring them to prove they deserve it, is a sure-fire way to kill love and unity in almost any group. But if disharmony is your objective, never forgive, never forget. It's fool-proof.

Step Seven: Hide your own sin behind harsh attitudes.

A number of years ago a well-known evangelist admitted he had been involved in a battle with lust. He had never been involved with another woman in any immoral activity, but his thought life had been plagued with unhealthy images and desires.

By his own admission, he had railed against sexual sin to hide his own problem: "I was trying to shout [lust] out of my life."

Now please understand—it's never wrong to denounce sin. But when our harsh denunciations of others is used to camouflage our own sin, it's wrong. Certainly this was the case with the Pharisees in Jesus' day, "Woe to you, teachers of the law and Pharisees, you hypocrites! You clean the outside of the cup and dish, but inside they are full of greed and self-indulgence" (Matt. 23:25).

Outwardly they looked good, but inwardly they conspired to kill Jesus. Aren't we all susceptible to the curious temptation of judging others by external standards to make ourselves look good?

If you wish to divide a congregation, take a beautiful truth of Scripture and take it to an extreme. Pronounce judgment on everyone who doesn't meet your external standards for righteousness.

The story is told of two men who happened to sit next to each other on a city bus one day. One noticed that the other was reading his Bible.

"Are you a Christian?" the first man asked.

"I certainly am," he said.

"Which church do you attend?"

"I attend First Pilgrim Brethren Church."

"You're kidding! I'm a member of the Third Pilgrim Brethren Church."

"Really!" said the other. "Are you part of the Nebraska Reformed Pilgrim Brethren denomination?"

"Yes, we are."

"That would make you a member of the American Conference of the Nebraska Reformed Pilgrim Brethren denomination?"

"Absolutely!"

"Unbelievable, to meet a brother like you in such a large city," said the second man.

"I assume you must also participate in the Twice Annual United American Conference of the Nebraska Reformed Pilgrim Brethren?" said the first man.

"Just came back from there last week as a matter of fact," said the other.

"This is too good to be true. What are the chances of meeting someone else from the Western Twice Annual American Conference of the Nebraska Reformed Pilgrim Brethren on a busy bus like this?"

There was a long pause. "Uh, I'm afraid you have it wrong," said the second man. "I'm a member of the *Eastern* Twice Annual American Conference of the Nebraska Reformed Pilgrim Brethren."

"You're what?" shouted the first man. "You're Eastern?" He got up out of his seat and stormed to the back of the bus. "I'd rather be caught dead than with a heretic like you!"

One of Satan's primary strategies is to convince believers that other believers are the enemy. To the extent he succeeds in convincing us that other Christians are the problem, he will be free to work his malevolent will in the world.

I don't need to remind you that while Lenin and the Bolsheviks were swarming in the streets of Russia in 1917 to stage a Communist coup, the members of the official church met in session to heatedly debate the proper length of altar candles.

The time has come to reexamine our motives and the true cost of judging other Christians. It is far too high.

But if you wish to divide a local church, simply take precious and important truths, wrap them in legalistic behavior and harsh attitudes, then whip your opponents with them until the blood runs down the aisle. It will not only give the infidels what they deserve, it will silence the convicting voice of God in your own life.

Step Eight: Use prayer to unite discontented individuals (and spread inappropriate information).

Are you looking for the perfect pretext to recruit other discontented people like you? Let me suggest a method that will not only cover your tracks, but will give the appearance you are a spiritually concerned and mature believer. Start a prayer meeting or small group, preferably in your home or the home of another disgruntled church member, to use as a cover to complain about the pastor or others in the church.

Serve refreshments. Perhaps even sing a chorus or hymn. A brief Bible study might also help. But then get down to the real business of the night. Discuss the pastor's obvious faults and the lack of true leadership in the congregation. Share stories with one another that illustrate the worst in others.

When you catch your kids listening around the corner, shoo them away. If they insist on knowing what you're doing, tell them you're having a "very important meeting."

Should the tone of the gathering start to become too ugly or critical for the faint at heart among you, refocus the remainder of the meeting on taking prayer requests. That will keep those who are less stalwart from getting up to leave.

Now what type of prayer requests should you solicit? Let me offer a suggestion or two:

"Let's pray for Pastor Jones, that God will help him get his ego back under control."

"Pray for Sheila, she just got fired again because her supervisor smelled alcohol on her breath after lunch."

"We should remember our elder chairman. He has a lot to contend with now that his wife is in clinical depression."

"I'd like you to pray for Bruce. He says he's about to quit as treasurer because of the way the youth pastor handles money."

These, of course, are not the only type of prayer requests that can be used to embarrass, belittle, or demean others in the church. But they do illustrate the basic principles of taking something holy and using it for an unholy purpose. Here then are the basic rules for a rump group:

1. Share information no one else in the room has any right to know.

2. Discuss details that can't be immediately verified or denied by anyone else in the room.

3. Reveal just enough facts to leave a questionable impression of another person's character.

One of the most painful stories I ever read was by a former pastor driven from his church by a group that used the tactics I suggested above. Listen to the things that had been "shared" about him in small groups. Eventually the stories left him and his wife too heartbroken to continue in ministry. As you read this, try to imagine the pain you would feel if people said similar things about you and your family.

One day a neighbor stopped me in the grocery store and said, "I'm sorry to hear about your David."

"What do you mean?" I asked.

"His arrest for doing drugs and selling them."

"Where did you hear this?"

"A member of your church told me."

Another time I saw a friend as I walked in the park.

"It's good to see you're doing better," he said. "You were in the hospital under suicide watch, weren't you?"

Old friends and colleagues would see me in public and be surprised that I seemed to be functioning like a normal human being. Fay (my wife) ran into old neighbors who expressed concern over something that was supposed to have happened to her—like her husband leaving her for another woman.[1]

How does damaging, if not slanderous, information such as this get spread? Sometimes over the phone, other times over coffee, but sad to say, all too often in a small group assembled to "share concerns and pray."

Small groups are a vibrant and exciting place to experience spiritual refreshment, growth, and accountability. They are being used of God in marvelous ways across our nation. But they can be subverted, and when they are, the results can be devastating to a church.

There is an Old Testament warning that is repeated twice in the Scriptures, once in 1 Chronicles 16:22, and again in Psalm 105:15. Both times it reads, "Do not touch my anointed ones; do my prophets no harm."

The principle behind that warning is this, "Don't take into your own hands the right to injure a servant of God." There is certainly a sense in which every believer is a servant of God, but there is also a sense in which pastors and church leaders are set apart for special service to God.

So before you consider assembling a group of discontented and angry church members to "pray" about the shortcomings and faults of your leaders, remember the Lord's warning, "Do not touch my anointed ones."

Why? Shouldn't we hold our leaders accountable? Of course we should. But we are not in the place of God, nor are we fit to judge another person's motives. It is also dangerous to take sacred things and use them for indecent purposes. To take the gift of prayer and use it as a forum to share mean-spirited and embarrassing information about another believer is something approaching sacrilege.

It's not too different from a problem that existed in the early church at Corinth. Instead of getting together to celebrate the Lord's supper, certain people saw it as an occasion to binge on food and get howling drunk. Listen to Paul's warning, "A man ought to examine himself before he eats of the bread and drinks of the cup. For anyone who eats and drinks without recognizing the body of the Lord eats and drinks judgment on himself. That is why many among you are weak and sick, and a number of you have fallen asleep" (1 Cor. 11:28-30).

God doesn't take lightly the abuse of worship settings, small fellowship groups, or Bible study sessions for selfish and immoral purposes. He knows that is destructive to the well-being of believers and the health of his church.

Fortunately, there are believers who refuse to participate in such grumble groups. On one occasion I received a phone call from a person concerned about the recent actions of his pastor. After listening for a few moments, it sounded as if the potential existed for underground groups and gossip to get started.

"Frank," I said, "whatever your concerns are, you must take the high road. Don't go behind the pastor with these issues. Jesus said we are go to our brother and show him his fault. You need to meet with the pastor and the appropriate leadership to discuss these issues. Do the right thing in the right way, and I believe God will honor you for it."

Frank was a person of high character. He took the high road, and eventually the situation was resolved.

But if you're goal is to divide the church and leave long-lasting scars and create spiritual paralysis, use prayer and small group discussions to wash the dirty laundry. It won't be long until everyone is up to their necks in foul tub water.

Step Nine: Do whatever you have to do to win.

During the Gulf War we witnessed a type of warfare we had not seen in fifty years. We watched a tyrant fire missiles at random into civilian populations with the hope of killing as many people as possible. He also used deadly chemical gas to try and exterminate minorities in his own country. His occupying forces ransacked cities, and in some cases they pulled intravenous tubes out of the arms of hospital patients. When it was clear Saddam Hussein had been defeated, he ordered his retreating armies to dynamite the remaining oil wells in Kuwait. That directive created a hellish inferno and a near ecological disaster.

There's now reasonable suspicion that either exposure to chemical warfare agents or prolonged exposure to the toxic oil fumes has led to "Gulf War Syndrome." That's the name of a strange disease that afflicts as many as twenty thousand American service personnel who fought in that war. What Hussein did was to adopt a strategy of "total war."

"Total war" is using every means available to you, regardless of how ruthless or immoral it is, to defeat your opponent. If you're aim is to split a congregation, I suggest you adopt a total war strategy. That will give you complete freedom to drive your opponent(s) out of the church, out town, and perhaps out of the ministry for good.

But if you profess to be a Christian, you will need some justification for your ruthless behavior. Let me suggest you try using some prooftexts. Now, you can't find Scripture verses to justify total war in the church because they don't exist. But if you're willing to take verses out of context (a small price to pay to get the Bible on your side), let me suggest you try these for starters:

"Expel the wicked man from among you" (1 Cor. 5:13).

"And one of them struck the servant of the high priest, cutting off his right ear" (Luke 22:50).

"I have nothing but hatred for them; I count them my enemies" (Ps. 139:22).

Listen to one example of total war tactics that were used only moments before a worship service:

One Sunday morning, as I walked into the sanctuary to prepare for the worship service, I saw several individuals welcoming the arriving congregation by handing out flyers, urging them to sign the petition [for my removal].

I went out and said to one of them, "How can you do this to people who are coming here to worship and hear God's Word?"

"This is our church, not yours," one of them replied, "and it's about time you realized it!"

One of the deacons was making friendly small talk with those handing out flyers. I took him aside. "Do you expect me to lead worship and preach with this going on?"

The deacon, who loathed confrontation, replied, "Pastor, you have to understand these people..."

I was devastated. The guerrillas were attacking our most sacred event, and one of my officers tells me I need to understand these people.[2]

The pastor soon resigned and left the ministry.

How is it that members of the same local church can reach the point where they will resort to the lowest of tactics to achieve their goals? I agree with the man who wrote,

Rather than recognizing personal motivations and differences, we attribute evil motives to others. Church fights become struggles over right and wrong, good and evil, orthodoxy and heresy. Opponents are not merely antagonists but Satan's emissaries.

He goes on to describe the "baggage" people often bring with them from their troubled homes of origin.

> Because of their brokenness, many view us [pastors] as the parent they never had.... Warner White, an Episcopalian, notes that when members "become stuck in...disillusion, the [pastor] becomes the symbol of antichrist. 'We thought he was the messiah, but he is just the opposite!' The [pastor] becomes the symbol of betrayal at the most profound level."[3]

Of course, waging total war in the congregation is a direct violation of how we are told to act toward one another in the church of Jesus Christ. "Be kind and compassionate to one another, forgiving each other, just as in Christ God forgave you" (Eph. 4:32).

But if you're willing to ignore certain passages of Scripture and take others out of context, there's a good case to be made that you should do whatever you have to do to win.

Step Ten: Remember, you are on a mission from God.

The final step in splitting a church is to declare that you are taking divisive steps because God told you to. If you claim a special directive from heaven, you can effectively remove yourself from all accountability to the church or anyone else. Who would dare question God?

Some of the most repulsive crimes in society are committed by those who claim to be on a special mission from God. We usually identify these individuals as the sick people they truly are. Jim Jones is just one example. It is sad that they drag God's name into their psychotic behaviors.

But not everyone who claims to have a special message from God resorts to violence. A Chicago newspaper carried the story of a religious group who sincerely believed God directed them to let all the air out of people's tires as an act of worship. They would charge out to cars stopped at intersections or parked by sidewalks and deflate all four tires. Apparently they believed heaven will be free of Goodyear radials.

Chances are you or I will never encounter anyone in the local church that bizarre. But in the midst of a severe church split, people will often do strange things and claim they are acting on God's behalf.

A friend of mine preached at a church one morning that was in the midst of a difficult controversy. He had no sooner offered the benediction when a young woman charged into the sanctuary and threw herself down at the front of the church.

"God, deliver us from this wicked pastor!" she cried out. "His sin cries out for your vengeance. Judge him before it's too late." Two women had to lead her out of the sanctuary.

Not all Sunday morning protests are that dramatic. Consider the pastor who found a leaflet on the floor of the sanctuary after a morning service:

"RESTORE COMMUNITY CHURCH TO ITS HIS-TORY OF BIBLICAL INTEGRITY!" it said in flaming red headlines. "REMOVE PASTOR WELLS!"

Brian groaned reflexively, as if he'd been punched in the stomach.

"Brian Wells is bent on imposing his liberal views on our church," the leaflet explained. "His utter disregard for the inspiration of Scripture will tear Community Church from its cherished biblical moorings—unless we act now..."

Brian scanned down, looking for something identifying who wrote it, but the paper ended only with the words "ACT NOW!"[4]

The person who printed the inflammatory, anonymous leaflet obviously thought he was acting on God's behalf to rid the church of an infidel. He was above accountability; he was taking his orders directly from God.

Why should you claim you are on a special mission from God? Let me suggest some of the practical benefits:

1. You can ignore all the rules, committees, and structures that exist in the church.

If you are on a special mission from God you don't have to follow established procedures. This frees you up to use any means or tactics you desire to accomplish your purposes. You don't have to produce credible evidence to back up your claim, verify information, or face appropriate boards with your accusations.

2. You can shame your opponents into silence.

If someone does happen to raise the question, "How do you know God told you to do it?" you simply reply, "If you were walking closer with God, you'd learn to listen for instructions."

3. Finally, your claim is beyond verification.

Who can possibly dispute that God told you to do what you are doing? Admittedly, few people actually go to such extremes to get their way in a local church. But individuals in a nasty church fight will say, "God told me to..."

Ed Dobson, pastor of Calvary Church in Grand Rapids, Michigan, refuses to say, "God told me to do this." When making a decision, he prefers to say, "At this time this is what I believe the best course of action is."

Do I believe that God still speaks to the hearts of his people? Of course I do. His Word and Spirit are at work. You only have to look at the amazing ministry going on around the world in Bible translation, missions work, evangelism on college and university campuses, efforts to rebuild the family, and a host of other ministries to know God is in the vision-building business.

And do I believe that God directs us in the particular events of our lives? Of course I do. Then why am I hesitant to say, "God told me so." The answer is found in Jeremiah 17:9, "The heart is deceitful above all things and beyond cure. Who can understand it?" It is far too easy for us to believe we are hearing the voice of God when all we are hearing is our own subconscious selfish desires telling us what to do.

I once knew a person who wasn't terribly fond of hard work. Every time there was a work day where walls needed scrubbing, toilets needed cleaning, and floors needed polishing, Steve would show up and then just disappear. Just about the time we would break for lunch, we'd find Steve kneeling in the sanctuary. "I just felt I needed to spend some time in prayer," he'd explain. Actually, he needed an excuse to get out of some nasty jobs. But who could question a man's call to prayer?

Another reason it's dangerous to say, "God told me to do this," is that the voice may indeed come from a spirit, but not the Spirit of God.

Neil Anderson, author of *The Bondage Breaker*, tells the story of a young man in seminary who was experiencing emotional and physical problems. When Anderson asked him how these strange symptoms started, the student explained, "Every day before I eat lunch, I ask God where I should go. He usually directs to Burger King or somewhere else. Lately, he's been directing me to attend a Mormon church."[5]

It is possible not only to deceive ourselves, but to be deceived by our adversary, the devil. The Bible tells us quite plainly, "Dear friends, do not believe every spirit, but test the spirits to see whether they are from God, because many false prophets have gone out into the world" (1 John 4:1).

There is an exception to the rule of not claiming you are on a mission from God, and that's when you follow Jesus' directive found in the Sermon on the Mount: "Blessed are the peace-makers, for they will be called sons of God" (Matt. 5:9).

If you really desire to have the blessing and backing of God in the midst of a conflict, adopt the role of a peacemaker. Expend your entire efforts on restoring grace and truth and unity to the church. Put away your selfish interests, hidden agendas, and need for control. If you do all this, you can indeed say you're on a mission from God.

Otherwise, stifle yourself. God is not on the side of the group who wants teal blue carpet rather than beige in the sanctuary, nor does he favor gravel over asphalt in the new parking lot. Rather, he's on the side of those who seek to "keep the unity of the Spirit through the bond of peace."

But if you're goal is to split your church right down the middle, then defend your every position with the claim, "God told me to say or do this." You will most certainly alienate others, remove yourself from accountability, and leave lasting scars on the body of believers.

Conclusion

There you have it. The top ten secrets of splitting a local church. Actually, they aren't much of a secret. They've been used in church fights for just about as long as the church has been in existence. My hope is that in reviewing them, we all might see how destructive our actions can be when our pride, anger, and need for power blinds us to what we are doing.

While I was in college, I was invited to serve on the administrative board of my church. After one meeting that had turned particularly nasty, I did something that was quite unusual for me— I began to weep. My heart was broken by what I had witnessed.

One of the board members approached me afterward as I had my head bowed. He cleared his throat, "Uh, Bob, I'm sorry about what happened tonight. Sometimes in the middle of an argument, even Christians can tend to get carried away."

I looked up at him and he must have seen the tears in my eyes. I appreciated his comments, but the only one who seemed to know what to do was my dad, who was also a member of the board. He walked over and simply put his arm around me. "Take as long as you need to, son," he said. I suspect I wasn't the only one who wept that night. The problem is, tears in heaven can't be seen.

Notes

1. Andre Bustanoby, "Wars You Can't Win," *Leadership Journal* 14 (Winter 1993):62.

2. Ibid., 61.

3. Arlo Walker, "Are Pastors Abused?" *Leadership Journal* 14 (Winter 1993):81-82.

4. Edward G. Dobson, Speed B. Leas, and Marshall Shelley, *Mastering Conflict and Controversy* (Portland, Ore.: Multnomah Press, 1992), 175.

5. Neil Anderson, *The Bondage Breaker* (Eugene, Ore.: Harvest House Publishers, 1990), 53-54.

CHAPTER 5

The Gallery

Conflict experts tell us the majority of conflicts in the church directly involve the pastor. Three common errors occur: (1) the pastor overreacts and attempts to over control the situation, (2) the pastor avoids conflict until it becomes unmanageable, or (3) the pastor manages church conflict well but neglects the tensions and problems in his personal life and family. In each situation, the church and the pastor are headed for serious trouble.

"I'm worried, John. It's just too big a risk to take this church," said Lori, John's wife. "I think we should stay right where we are."

John paced the length of the deluxe hotel room and rubbed his neck. "I hear what you're saying, but there's so many things I like about the church."

John stopped and stared out the large window on the twelfth floor. Outside the sun had set and now the bright lights of the city began to flicker on, creating a universe of street-level stars. "Lord, what should we do?" John said out loud.

Lori walked up behind him and rubbed his shoulders.

"John, I'm not trying to tell you whether or not you should take Westminster Chapel. But I think we need to take a close look at its track record. Only one pastor has stayed more than eight years, and his marriage fell apart. Doesn't that concern you?"

The middle-aged pastor turned around and put his arms around his wife.

"Lori, I've always trusted your instincts. I'm not going any further in this candidating process until we have our questions answered. You're right, I could easily become just another oil portrait in the hallway."

Lori laid her head on John's shoulder.

"I wish I knew what to say, John. We're happy where we are now. I just don't see why we should leave."

"Look," he smiled, "it's getting late and we have a breakfast meeting with the search committee early in the morning. Let's sleep on it. Things might be clearer to us in the morning."

That night John tossed and turned. Part of his restlessness had to do with the uncomfortable hotel mattress that sloped to one side. But most of his insomnia was plain old stress. He knew one bad decision could ruin his career and his family.

He propped up his pillow and put his hands behind his head. "Please let me get some rest, Lord," he prayed quietly. "I need to be able to think clearly and make a good decision."

He looked over at the glowing green numbers on the radio alarm clock—12:57 A.M. "Good grief, I can't believe how late it already is." He rolled over and buried his face in his pillow. A few minutes later he was sound asleep and drifted into his dreams.

The next thing Pastor John knew, he stood in the corridor of Westminster Chapel staring at the oil portraits of the former pastors. The search committee chairman had told him that all the former pastors, with the exception of one man, had left the ministry. He had a church in a retirement community in Arkansas. The next pastor now managed a local bookstore. The last pastor had taken a job as a stockbroker.

John walked down the row of faces and stared at the first portrait. It was a picture of the founding pastor of Westminster

Chapel. The man was dressed in a gray, three-piece suit and horn-rimmed glasses. Underneath the portrait, a gold nameplate indicated his years of service: "Reverend James B. McDuffy, 1974-79."

"So what should I do, Mr. McDuffy?" John said in a whisper. "Should I accept a call to this church or not?"

"I can't make that decision for you," came the reply. John took a step back. He thought he had heard a voice.

"I didn't get enough sleep last night," John said to himself. "The stress must be getting to me. I'd better find Lori." He looked up and down the hall. "Lori," he called out. She was nowhere to be found.

"For the moment it's just you and me," said the portrait in front of him.

"But...but..." John began backing away from the portrait.

"You asked me a question, so I'll answer it," said the portrait. "It seems the only courteous thing to do." The stern expression on the oil canvas had changed to one that was a bit more pleasant.

Whoa. I need to find Lori and call a cab, John thought. *Now pictures are actually talking to me.*

"Calm down, man. Steady," McDuffy said. "I might be able to help you."

"But you're just a picture...on a wall...made of canvas. And portraits don't talk to people."

"John, let me tell you a little about myself," said McDuffy, chuckling a bit. "I started this church in the early 1970s." The old gentleman took off his glasses and cleaned them with the starched white handkerchief from his front coat pocket.

"I was much younger then. Actually I was about thirty-eight when I planted this church," continued McDuffy. "The denomination was looking for someone with determination, grit. Someone who could move into this community and establish a solid church." He laughed quietly to himself again. "That's when they turned to me."

Curiosity replaced shock in John, so he took a step closer to the picture. "So...so they asked you to come here?"

"That's right, young man. I was promised just fifty dollars a week of support from the denomination, the rest I had to take on faith. We started out in a clothing store that had been through a fire. We bought it for a song. Worked night and day for three months to restore the building. Held our first service in what used to be the men's suit department. On hot days you could still smell the smoke."

"Did you do most of the work yourself?" John asked.

"Absolutely, young man," McDuffy said, his thick eyebrows coming together in sincerity. "In those days we had unity. Real unity. I mean everyone pulled together. Men and women gave their evenings to come and scrape walls. Paint floors. Carry out trash. Giving went up every month."

"The people had a cause, a reason to pull together," said John.

"Yup. Before I knew it, we were running 250 people on a Sunday morning," said McDuffy, a hint of pride in his voice. "We quit accepting denominational support after just five months. No one at headquarters could believe it. The second year we started Sunday evening services. By the third year we funded our first missionaries. The Beaumonts. Fine people. Went to Borneo if I remember right."

"So why did you just stay"—John looked down at the inscription under the portrait—"why did you just stay six years?"

The look of pride and satisfaction on the older pastor's face suddenly disappeared. "Because of Kadesh Barnea," he replied, a look of anger now glistening in his eyes.

"Kadesh Barnea? Who...what are you talking about?"

"Didn't they teach you anything in seminary?" McDuffy said.

John could feel his neck turning red with embarrassment. He scanned his memory to try and remember Kadesh Barnea. "They sound like two Hebrew words to me. Maybe they're—"

"Since you obviously don't remember, I'll refresh your memory," interrupted McDuffy. "Kadesh Barnea is where the children of Israel refused to enter the Promised Land. They were talked out of receiving their inheritance by a group of cowardly, unbelieving, spineless spies who claimed the land was crawling with giants."

The light went on in John's memory. "Sure, now I remember," he said. "Moses had sent out the twelve spies, and only Joshua and Caleb came back and said, 'We can do it. We can take the land.' "

"My faith in seminaries is a bit restored," McDuffy huffed. The older gentleman took off his glasses and pointed them straight at John's face. "And if the board had listened to me we could have built the largest building in the district! We would have been running a thousand people on Sundays. But no, instead they voted to build a building half the size of what we needed. That's when I preached The Sermon."

"The Sermon?" John said.

"That's right, young man. When the building committee opposed me, I decided to take my case to the people. May 8, 1979. That's the morning I preached The Sermon."

"What may I ask, was The Sermon?"

"Then you haven't heard about it?" asked McDuffy. He sounded more disappointed than irritated.

"I'm afraid not, sir."

"Then I'll tell you. My wife, Emma, told me not to do it, but I chose to ignore her. I knew it was time for this congregation to fish or cut bait. I spent the entire week preparing just what I wanted to say. Yes sirree, I didn't mince words that morning."

"What was you text?"

"I used the story of the twelve spies Moses had sent out. I compared our congregation to the children of Israel. We had wandered long enough in the wilderness. It was time for us to seize the moment and enter the Promised Land. And the Promised Land to us was building a thousand-seat church on a parcel of property I had found on the edge of town. God had told me we ought to buy that property, and like Moses, I didn't dare disobey."

John didn't need to ask, but wanted to confirm his suspicions, "And the twelve spies? Did they happen to correlate with the twelve members on your board?"

"Have you heard this story from someone else? You said you hadn't."

"No, it was a lucky guess. Please, go on."

"You're sure you haven't heard this before. I hate to waste my time repeating things someone else already knows."

"No," John said. "This is all news to me." *Wait until Lori hears about this.*

"In any case, I finished The Sermon by declaring, 'Today, I wish for us to learn who are the Joshuas and Calebs among us. We must also learn who are the faithless and fearful. I am going to read the names of the twelve members of the board. Those in favor of inheriting the promises God has made us—buying the property and building the building we need—please come up here and stand to my right. Those who intend to hold us back from realizing our dream—come up here and stand to my left.'"

"You actually said that in a Sunday morning service?" John asked.

"You bet your bottom dollar I did."

"What...what happened?"

"Well, sir, I read the list of the board members one by one. At first, they were reluctant to get up. But I refused to back down. It was high time the congregation saw what these men were made of. One person was home sick that morning, so there were just eleven men in the service. All I needed was a simple majority of the board."

"Did you get it?"

"Just hold on. The first man got up and stood to my right. So did the next one. But the third man, he got up and stood to the left. So did the next four men. But then two more took my side. That left just one man. Stuart was his name. The deciding vote. He sat there, head bowed, for the longest time."

"Weren't you taking an awful risk?" John asked.

"To win big, you need to be willing to lose big," said McDuffy. "I looked at Stuart and said, 'Frank, do you want be remembered as a Joshua or as one of the cowards? Do you want this day in our church's history to go down as a Jericho victory or as Kadesh Barnea, a place of stubborn refusal to believe God for his promises?' "

"What did the man say?"

"He got up slowly, a pained look on his face, then he walked up the center aisle. He stood in between the two groups. 'What's it going to be?' I said. 'Enough waffling.' He finally looked up at me and said, 'Pastor, I wish you weren't forcing me to do this. Not here, not now. I can't see anything good coming from dividing the board over something like this. Why don't we all go home and give this more thought and prayer?' But I would hear none of it. It was the hour of decision. I wasn't about to let him weasel out of taking a stand."

"So what happened?" said John.

The older gentleman looked down, a hint of sadness filled his voice. "Stuart stood and prayed for about two minutes, then walked over to the group on the left. 'Are you declaring yourself against me?' I demanded. 'I'm not against you, pastor,' he said. 'But we don't have the funds to build. Not yet. God may have indeed told you we need the building, but he hasn't told all the rest of us yet.' "

The bitterness of that defeat was etched in the face of Pastor McDuffy.

"Did you decide to table the matter?" John asked.

"I did not!" shouted McDuffy. "I declared to the congregation that if they would not follow me into the Promised Land, they would have to find another Moses to lead them. I resigned right then and there and walked off the stage."

"But...but didn't that cause a division in the congregation?"

"They were already divided! Sunday, May 8, that's the day this Westminster Chapel became Kadesh Barnea."

"Did any others leave with you?" John asked.

"The bold of heart did," he answered. "There was a hastily called board meeting after the service. They sent a delegation to suggest I should reconsider my resignation, but I refused. By June the congregation was half its size. Serves them right," McDuffy muttered.

"I don't mean to sound impertinent, sir," said John. "But wasn't there any other way to resolve the issue?"

"So, you're one of them too," said McDuffy. "Let me give you some advice, young man. If you can't stand the heat, get out of the kitchen. The church doesn't need more mealy-mouthed compromisers who try and please everyone. They need people willing to take a stand. Willing to take their losses. This congregation got just what it deserved."

"But at what cost?" John asked. "The church split in half and you resigned. It strikes me that the cure was worse than the disease."

"That's the trouble with this generation—no spine, no guts," said McDuffy. "When you're in the Lord's work you play for keeps. Can't you understand that? Whose side are you on? Tell me. Whose side?...Whose side?..."

The corridor grew quiet for a moment as McDuffy's voice died out.

"He left me with a real mess," said the next picture. John turned his attention away from the first portrait to the second one. It was the face of a much smaller, younger man. John walked over and squinted to read the inscription under his portrait. "Reverend Paul Allison, 1981-86."

John glanced over at McDuffy's portrait. He had resumed his stern, unyielding, still-life pose.

"You couldn't believe the confusion and pain when I arrived," said the next portrait. By now John was accustomed to these oil paintings conversing, so he walked over and stood in front of the canvas. The pastor looked to be quite young; he wore a well-trimmed beard.

John realized he was staring at the man and that was rude. "I'm sorry," said John. "I'm John Harrington, a possible candidate for senior pastor here."

"I've been listening the last several days," said Allison. "They gave me much the same pitch when I was a candidate. But before you make up your mind, you might want to know a little more history about this place."

"I'd appreciate that," said John. "It's a big decision."

"I wish I had taken more time. See, I had a small church in Wisconsin. It was doing fine. That's when I heard about this opportunity. I couldn't believe a church the size of Westminster would be interested in me. I guess I leaped before I looked." The young man reached up and loosened his tie.

"So you regret coming here?" said John.

"Let's just say it was my final church. I decided after eight years here I might be more suited to the business world. So I took a job at a Christian bookstore."

"You followed McDuffy, didn't you? I notice by the dates that there was almost two years between pastors."

"You're very observant, John. It took the better part of two years for the church even to be able to agree on a pastor. They decided after McDuffy they needed more a lover than a fighter. That's why they called me."

"I would imagine you were well-received," said John. "I mean, you sound like a much more gentle person than..." he pointed over to McDuffy's portrait.

"Than him?" said Allison. "Sure, at first everyone treated me like a hero. They said how nice it was to have a pastor that would listen and not insist on his way. They liked the fact I rarely said what I thought about things. I came here with the idea that the board was my boss and I would take my orders from them."

"Didn't that make for peace and a time of healing at Westminster?"

"At first. In fact, after three years we began to grow again. That's when we decided to eventually relocate. This time there was no division about relocating and building. Everyone was anxious to get over their reputation as, 'Kadesh Barnea.' "

"So why didn't it work? You listened to others. You rarely shared your own opinions. You let the board have their way. No church fights."

At the mention of "church fights," Allison appeared to wince.

"It was a time of peace, wasn't it?" asked John.

"For a season," said Allison. "It was until...the conflict with the choir director."

"What happened?"

"Music became a big part of Westminster after we got into our new building. The board decided to call someone as a music and choir director full-time. Personally, I felt like we needed someone full-time in youth ministry. But I didn't want to make a big fuss, so I just went along with it. They ended up hiring Steven Bensen, a music major from the university."

"He sounds well qualified."

"Actually he was a perfectionist. He liked classical music,

oratorios, things like that. But a lot of our young people weren't really into that. What's more, he announced to me one day that he would choose the hymns on Sunday morning, not me."

"So you told him you were in charge of the worship service?" asked John.

"I tried to tell him it was important that I have a say in the service so it fit with my sermon, but he told me I was uneducated in music and I should stay out of his realm."

"That sounds like insubordination to me," said John. "After all, you were the senior pastor."

"But the Bible says the Lord's servant should not quarrel, and as much as possible, be at peace with all people."

"But there's a difference between a quarrelsome spirit and the right to exercise legitimate authority," said John. "After all, the Bible also says to pay double honor to those who preach and teach."

Allison looked depressed. "Look, I don't know if you can appreciate where I'm coming from or not. But when I was a boy, I grew up in an alcoholic home. My dad would threaten my mom. I tried to keep peace. I hated conflict. See, when people fight, everyone gets hurt. Okay?"

"I didn't mean to offend you," said John.

"It wasn't easy being here," Allison's voice began to rise. "I mean it was one thing after another. Two teachers got in a fight over who could use classroom space. They both came storming into my office and demanded I make the decision. I told them it wasn't my area of responsibility. Then came the doctrine blow-up. Two elders got in an argument over the meaning of the Lord's Supper. One was really into a guy on the radio. Before I knew it they refused to serve communion together on Sundays. I told them to just forget about this issue, that we had more important things to worry about."

"Did you ever teach on the subject?"

"No, I thought it would look like I was taking sides. Pastors aren't supposed to take sides. We're supposed to love everyone."

"Loving people can also include drawing boundaries and taking scriptural stands, particularly on an issue that people look to you for help on," John said. "I had to face the same thing a few years ago when people got into an argument over the timing of Christ's return."

"I probably could have survived that battle if the youth group crisis hadn't hit the same year," said Allison. "I got word from a parent that one of the youth sponsors, a guy in his early thirties, was spending a lot of time alone with one of the girls from the high school group."

"Did you check it out?"

"What? And make it look like I was suspicious of the man? I told the mother that unless she had positive proof there was hanky-panky going on, I didn't want to hear about it. The Bible says we are to avoid gossip."

"How did you know it was gossip?" asked John innocently.

Allison chose to ignore his question. "So two months later I get a call at 2:00 A.M. on a Saturday. This sponsor and this high school gal are spotted coming out of a bar together. They went off in his car."

"Were they dating?"

"He was married at the time. Everything broke loose after that. He admitted he had been involved in an affair with her. Divorced his wife. The parents sued the church—and me."

"So what did you do?"

"I had had enough of local church ministry. A friend of mine from college had just opened a bookstore in the city. He needed a manager so I took the job. That's the thanks I got for trying to keep the peace."

The irony of the moment wasn't lost on John. Allison and McDuffy had something in common. Though they were diametrically opposed in their philosophy of ministry and leadership, they had both left the church angry and bitter.

"I'm...I'm sorry," said John. "It sounds like it was a very difficult period of your life."

"I just let them find another whipping boy," said Allison. "By then I had had it with the local church. For good." He fought back tears.

"Hey, you gave it your best shot." Even as John said the words, he knew he didn't mean it. Allison had run from every conflict until finally there was nowhere to hide.

"Paul brought healing to the church when they needed it," said another voice. John jerked his head in the direction of the third and final portrait. It was a man in his forties with dark brown hair combed straight back, a definite tan, and ocean blue eyes. He wore a pin-striped suit with a contemporary tie.

"Who are you?" said John.

"I'm Steve Bartello-Bergren," he said in a pleasant voice. The inscription beneath him read, "Reverend Steven C. Bartello, 1986-94."

"Your name's slightly different than what's on this portrait," said John.

"That's right, I changed it when I married Samantha last year," said the handsome pastor.

What am I thinking? John said to himself. *The search committee told me on the phone that the last pastor's wife had filed for divorce.* It was an awkward moment. "So where are you living now?" asked John.

"Sam and I live along the coast. She works as a marketing rep for an international pharmaceuticals company and I'm a stock broker." His natural charisma and easy smile seemed to hide the faint sound of sadness in his voice. "We're doing great."

"Would you mind if I asked you about the church? I'm a possible candidate to follow you here," said John.

"Hey, go ahead. I have nothing to hide."

"From all that I've heard, you really did a terrific job here."

"Thanks. After Paul Allison left we had some heavy-duty issues to clean up. We finally decided to let the choir director go. We lost a few folks over it, but we rode out the storm. Oh, and the communion issue. I led the elders though a year study on the subject, and we finally adopted a position paper. The two elders eventually reconciled. Fortunately we were able to settle the youth sponsor lawsuit out of court. Taught us an important lesson. Where's there's smoke, you owe it to the church to see if there's fire."

"Sounds like you handled things in a decisive way," said John. "I mean, you got most of the problems resolved."

"Yeah, I worked hard during my years at Westminster. Real hard. It wasn't unusual for me to put in seventy- or eighty-hour weeks."

"When did things finally stabilize around here?" asked John.

"Oh, I'd say about 1992. That's when we went into our third building program. I was also teaching part time at the seminary by then."

"I can see why you needed eighty hours in a week," said John. "Did anyone ever worry about how hard you were working?"

"Oh, they would warn me from time to time to slow down. But I knew deep down in their hearts they liked it. They had considered Allison a little bit of a slough-off."

"How about your w—" John stopped before he said the word. But Steve knew what he was asking.

"It's okay, we can talk about my first wife," said Steve. He looked away in thought for a moment. "Debbie and I had a good marriage. I know that seems hard to believe, but we really loved each other. We met in college. She was a pastor's daughter. We both felt called to the church. I knew I wanted to go on to seminary. So we got married. Didn't have much money in those days, but it didn't matter."

"Same here," said John. "There were nights in seminary when everyone on our floor would put their food together so we could have a meal."

"I hear you," said Steve. "Once we got out, things got better. Debbie worked as a nurse until Justin came along. Then we had Molly. I worked as an associate at a church of three thousand for ten years until Westminster opened up. This area was growing so we took the church."

"They still speak highly of you here, Steve," said John. He genuinely liked the man in the portrait.

"Thanks," he said. He brushed his nose with the back of his hand and looked away again. "Anyway, as the church grew, it seemed harder and harder for Debbie and me to have time together. On top of that Molly developed acute asthma. So Debbie was constantly having to take her in for treatments. I just couldn't get away."

"Steve, you don't have to share anything more of this with me. It's your own personal—"

"No, let me finish what I've started," said Steve. "It was a few years ago on Mother's Day. Can you believe it? Mother's Day. One of the elder's had invited me to play a round of golf with him in the afternoon. His wife had gone back East to visit her mother. So this guy was alone all day. He's a major CEO in the city. Fortune 500 and all that. So I asked Debbie if I could skip lunch and we'd do supper as a family. She said 'Sure, Steve. Whatever you want.'

"So when I got home I found the house empty. I go upstairs and her closet has been cleaned out. I find this note in the bathroom that she's leaving me and taking the kids. I thought she was kidding. When I got the papers the next week, I knew she wasn't."

"I'm sorry, Steve," said John.

"Hey, it happens, man. Besides, there's nothing I can do about it. Debbie got remarried about a year ago. That's when I met Samantha. We're doing okay."

It was obvious he still grieved the loss of his wife. "Hey, how about you? Are you going to take this church?"

"We're thinking about it," said John. "Lori and I haven't made up our minds yet. We're pretty happy where we are right now."

"Be careful, John. That's all I can say. I should have listened to the advice I got from one of the older men when I first came to Westminster Chapel."

"What was that?"

"He took me aside and said, 'Steve, you're a natural leader. The people like you. You know how to motivate others. But that may be your undoing. I've been in this church since McDuffy came, and I can assure you this church will allow you to work yourself to death. They'll cheer you right into your grave. Remember, Steve, no one will take care of you if you don't take care of yourself.'"

John didn't know what to say. Obviously the older gentleman's prophecy had come true. Steve gave so much to the church that he lost his marriage—and his ministry.

"So what do I do to protect myself?" John asked.

"Learn to say no to people. Work to live, don't live to work. Find two or three men you trust. Make yourself accountable to them for your marriage and work schedule. Don't confuse your own ego needs with the kingdom of God. Most importantly..."

"Yes?" said John.

"Remember that no one will take care of the pastor if you don't."

John swallowed hard. He knew he had the same predisposition to be a workaholic. He thrived on affirmation from others—almost too much. He found it hard to say no. Lori was always telling him to slow down and smell the flowers. Spend more time with her and the kids. "Steve, this is weird. I mean, here I am talking to an oil portrait and all. But could we make a deal?"

The figure inside the gold frame smiled. "Sure, buddy, what is it?"

"If I take this church, will you remind me every once in a while to take care of myself and my family? I mean, you're a class guy, and look what happened. You probably know this, but the church took your divorce really hard. The attendance is down, giving has fallen off, people are discouraged."

"I know," he mumbled. "I can still see the expressions on the face of the people the Sunday I resigned. They weren't angry. They weren't unforgiving. They were hurt. Deeply hurt. I'd give anything to have the last eight years over again." Tears ran down Steve's cheeks. He reached into his suit and retrieved a handkerchief. "Hey, I'm sorry, man. I didn't mean to do this."

"It's okay, Steve."

"No, it's not, John. I mean, I really didn't serve this church, I used it. I used it to feed my own ego. I used others. Debbie tried to tell me that but I just got angry at her. I let her and the kids become strangers." Steve took a long breath, then continued. "Funny, isn't it? When my kids lived at home I ignored them. Now that they're in Connecticut, all I do is think about them day and night. I guess you don't know what you have until you lose it, huh?"

"I guess not," John said in a quiet voice.

The next moment the canvas again became a still life. The portrait once again showed bright eyes, an easy smile, and dark brown hair combed straight back. The sad, empty, grieving face of Steve Bartello had disappeared.

Suddenly John remembered Lori. "I have to find her," he said out loud. He started down the hallway. "Lori? Lori, where are you?". He couldn't find her. Panic began to set it. "Lori! Please, where are you?"

"I'm right here, darling. What's wrong?"

John sat straight up. His face was covered with sweat. The hotel room was dark, but he noticed the green glow of the clock right next to him—2:35 A.M.

"Sweetheart, are you all right?" said his wife.

He turned and looked over at Lori. "Oh, thank you, Lord," he whispered out loud. "It was just a dream."

He laid his head back on the pillow.

"Was it a nightmare?" she asked.

"Depends on who you talk to," John said.

"What?"

"I'll tell you in the morning."

PART 2

How to Heal
Family Ties

CHAPTER 6

How Pastors
Can Bring Unity

I n the last chapter, we saw how three fictitious pastors all
reacted differently to stress and conflict in the church. One
was combative and competitive, the next passive and accom-
modating, and the third was consumed by his own ego needs. All
three approaches proved costly to the unity and harmony of the
church.

But the good news is that pastors can be a force for reconciliation and cooperation. They can model for their people how to
obey Christ and speak the truth in love. They can teach their
people how to handle conflict in mature and constructive ways.

For most of us, the process of learning to handle conflict is
just that—a learning process. Bill Hybels, pastor of Willow Creek
Community Church in South Barrington, Illinois, describes the
changes that took place in his own life that significantly
increased his effectiveness as a pastor:

> In my early years of ministry, I rebutted people who
> wrote to me and said I had offended them or hurt their
> feelings. For years, I'd write back and say essentially, "I'm

sorry you took it wrong, but there really wasn't anything wrong with what I said." But then they'd write back, doubly hurt. They knew what I really meant was, "I'm sorry you're so sensitive that you get upset about petty things."

After several years of this, I thought, *What if I just said, "Thank you for writing me and expressing your hurt. I'm sorry. I didn't intend to hurt you. Please forgive me."*

Soon after implementing this approach, I began receiving letters saying, "Thank you for your letter. You don't know how much that meant to me."

Many people, I discovered, just want to know if their pastor is a safe person. Can he respond to hurt with compassion? Does he care as much about relationships as he does his sermon material?... Our people already know we make mistakes. What they want to know is whether or not we have enough integrity to admit them.[1]

Because the majority of conflict in local churches takes place between a pastor and the congregation, it's important we look at the steps pastors can take to encourage unity and harmony. As Hybels says so well, "The mark of community—true biblical unity—is not the absence of conflict. It's the presence of a reconciling spirit."[2]

A Pastor with an Attitude—of Reconciliation

H. B. London defines reconciliation as "the restoration of friendship and fellowship after estrangement."[3] There are few times when a pastor's commitment to living out a spirit of reconciliation is as tested as when someone calls his character or motives into question. Consider this incident that Ben Patterson writes about:

I remember several years ago hearing a friend tell of a painful confrontation with a member of the church. The man had a list a mile long of criticisms aimed right at him as pastor. He had tried to use meals together as a means of reconciliation. All he had to show for his efforts however was heartburn.

The pastor felt bombarded by the number of smart-bomb questions and laser-guided accusations raining down on him. He interrupted the attack by saying to the gentleman, "Clearly, you think I'm doing everything wrong. But do you trust my heart?"

There was a long pause. The man looked at the pastor and said matter-of-factly, "No, I think you're trying to ruin the church."

The pastor was stunned. When he recovered he said, "No, wait. You really think that I am trying to destroy the church?"

"Yes," he replied. "I think you are."[4]

A Heart Exam for Pastors

While all believers have a responsibility to work toward true biblical unity, the Bible singles out the heart-attitudes and characteristics of pastors for special attention. That's the case in Paul's instructions to in his second letter to young pastor Timothy:

> [P]ursue righteousness, faith, love and peace, along with those who call on the Lord out of a pure heart. Don't have anything to do with foolish and stupid arguments, because you know they produce quarrels. And the Lord's servant must not quarrel; instead, he must be kind to everyone, able to teach, not resentful. Those who oppose him he must gently instruct, in the hope that God will

grant them repentance leading them to a knowledge of the truth, and that they will come to their senses and escape from the trap of the devil, who has taken them captive to do his will (2 Tim. 2:22-26).

Now, not everyone who opposes a pastor has been taken captive by the devil to do his will. The context of this passage suggests the captives were those who opposed sound doctrine and the truth of the gospel. But this paragraph does contain the basic truths a pastor must incorporate into his life to keep personal attacks and conflict from destroying his effectiveness.

Pursue Character, Not Control

What happens in us is more important to God than what happens to us. The development of a Christ-like character is God's first and foremost agenda for our lives. For that to happen, we sometimes go through difficult situations. It often means facing difficult critics and their scrutinizing assessments of our lives. Ben Patterson tells of his struggle between growing in character or reacting defensively:

> There was a woman in a church I served that could see little, if any, redeeming value in my ministry. As we were trying to work out the problem she told me that I had to be more receptive to what others wanted me to do (translated, it meant doing exactly what she wanted me to do).

> Instinctively, I reacted in exactly the opposite direction. I became determined to never give this woman control over my life or ministry. There was an element of truth to what she was saying, but my own ego strength sometimes wouldn't allow me to admit it. It's tempting to react by shutting someone out completely, writing them off as incorrigible cranks.

I find it difficult in those situations to readily forgive people. I know they need a model of Christ's love and forgiveness, but their actions eat away at my soul. Yet, if I don't follow Jesus' advice to bless those who persecute me, it will end up coming between God and me. That's too high of a price to pay.[5]

Patterson is describing the battle between character and control. Pastors have to choose between the two. Either I'm going to trust God that he is working out the maturing of my character by allowing me to face sometimes hostile critics, or I'm going to have to maneuver, plan, and manipulate to remove my critics from my life and ministry.

I remember hearing the story of a pastor who would tolerate no objection or opposition from his board. Whenever a board member or deacon would challenge him, he would call them into his office and say, "Jim, I've heard you're in opposition to what I'm doing."

"Yes, pastor, that's true. I am concerned about this area of the church's ministry."

The minister would then supposedly reply, "Well, sir, why don't we let the Lord decide who's right in this matter? Let's both pray that God will take home the one who's wrong in this situation." The pastor claimed that he had buried almost half a dozen deacons who were foolish enough to oppose the Lord's work (or him) and pray that prayer.

Whether the story is true or not, such an approach obviously isn't in keeping with the spirit of Paul's advice to Timothy, "pursue righteousness, faith, love, and peace, along with those who call on the Lord out of a pure heart." To ask God to strike dead the person who opposes you seems to suggest an insatiable need to control others.

There are, of course, more subtle methods of domination. We can quit talking to the grumbling parishioner, have them quietly removed from committees, criticize them to the other leaders, or openly humiliate them in a confrontation.

But only at a great cost to our character. To feed our appetite for control turns us ultimately into petty, vengeful, and ruthless individuals. It also destroys the inner character of the church. Instead of being a place of joy, vibrancy, and winsomeness, the church becomes a dwelling for suspicion, alliances, fear, and most of all, deep hurt.

But when we pursue righteousness, faith, love, peace, and a pure heart, even if we lose, we win.

Michelle Prentice-Leslie, pastor of a church in the suburban Chicago area, reminds us that we have to be sensitive to the loss and grief issues that are often behind the troublesome behavior of some individuals:

> People who have experienced a great loss in their lives may have difficulty letting go of the familiar, such as their role as choir director or trustee chair. The prospect of losing something else in their life that's been meaningful to them is too overwhelming. The result is they fight tooth and nail to hang on. [In those cases] I would share with the [person] some of the losses that have occurred in my own life. I'd admit these setbacks have made it difficult for me to entertain the idea of trying new things. I would explain how [their] own grief work may be adversely impacting their area of service and hindering the work of the Holy Spirit.[6]

When one of my harshest critics was hospitalized, my commitment to being a person of reconciliation was put to the test. Would I go and visit? Should I send someone else? It took all the mercy God could pour into my life for me to make the trip to the hospital and step in the elevator. I struggled as I walked down the corridor and entered the room. I was greeted with cold and unwelcome stares from the person's relatives as I walked in.

But after I had read Scripture and prayed with the individual, something changed inside me. I knew as I stepped back on the elevator that I was free—free from the need to punish or control that person. Free to love him.

Let me add a word of caution. The quest for character doesn't imply we roll over and become passive in the face of unjust and unfair criticism. It means that we respond by pursuing reconciliation with a loving and open heart. Hybels tells of one of the most painful accusations he ever had to deal with:

> Many years ago, I heard from reliable sources that a local pastor had commented repeatedly that Lynne and I were unhappily married, headed for divorce. Included in his charges were accusations of unfaithfulness. Needless to say, Lynne and I were deeply saddened by these false reports.
>
> After much discussion and prayer, Lynne and I drove to this pastor's church and walked into his office, unannounced, and introduced ourselves.
>
> "The things you have been saying have been ripping our hearts out," we said. "They're not true. We're wondering why you're saying what you're saying."
>
> "I thought my information was accurate," he sputtered. By the end of the conversation, he was apologetic. He appreciated that we had come to him and spoken the truth in a loving way. I think we all gained some valuable life lessons that day.[7]

By refusing the impulse to either run from the problem or run over his critic, Hybels was able to deal with a painful issue in a positive way. The pay-off of pursuing righteousness, faith, love,

peace, and a pure heart is that you eventually find them. They
take up residence in your soul.

Avoid the Irrelevant

As we've said in earlier chapters, there is a distinct difference
between moral absolutes, deeply held convictions, and personal
preferences. Pastors who are able to make those important differ-
entiations are far more likely to promote unity in their congregation.

My friend Linda once casually referred to the main auditorium
of a church as "the sanctuary." The person she was with immediately stiffened and said, "You mean the *auditorium*. We don't
believe in sanctuaries around here."

Linda could have picked up the challenge and engaged the
other person in a spirited theological argument over the correct
terminology for the room in which a congregation worships God.
The nature of the debate would not have been altogether irrelevant.

But there was an emotional hard edge to the person's voice,
almost an anger about the issue. As Linda read the situation, it
seemed the person was dealing with other issues in his life. So she
practiced some advice that the writer of Proverbs offers: "Starting
a quarrel is like breaching a dam; so drop the matter before a dispute breaks out" (Prov. 17:14). She smiled at the person and
changed the conversation to another topic. It wasn't worth dividing fellowship over.

My mother was part of a group that once got into a heated
discussion over whether to serve dill or sweet pickles for lunch.
Paul Cedar, the current president of the Evangelical Free Church,
remembers a congregational meeting he attended as a boy getting
ugly over whether to use brown or red shingles on the church's
roof. I've seen church boards melt down over who left mud on
the carpet.

What do all these incidents have in common? The issue that

led to division was irrelevant. Paul advises Timothy, "Don't have anything to do with foolish and stupid arguments, because you know they produce quarrels. And the Lord's servant must not quarrel" (2 Tim. 2:23-24).

As a general rule, it is best to major on the majors and minor on the minors. People who go through life seeing every issue in capital letters are going to frequently find themselves in conflict. When they consider every aspect of their faith as equivalent in value, the important is devalued and the trivial is exalted, and division results.

The Pharisees made that exact mistake. They would give to God a tenth of the smallest herbs in their garden, but rob the houses of widows. They would count the number of steps they walked on the Sabbath, but find ingenuous ways to get out of supporting aging parents.

Wouldn't it have been better for them to forget their endless rules and regulations and instead show mercy and kindness to others?

In the same fashion, it is far more important that we evidence the character of Christ than to enforce cultural and man-made rules and regulations in the local church. In recent years some churches have taken strong positions on issues such as the style of music used in worship, where children should be educated, and the proper size of a family. I honor the strong convictions these individuals hold. These are neither foolish nor insignificant matters. But it would be wrong to make any one of them a test of orthodoxy.

We are all one family, not because we all agree on matters such as these, but because, "There is one body and one Spirit—just as you were called to one hope when you were called—one Lord, one faith, one baptism; one God and Father of all, who is over all and through all and in all" (Eph. 4:4-6).

To promote unity and harmony, pastors need to avoid being

consumed in controversies and arguments that, in the light of eternity, will prove irrelevant in comparison to the important tasks of preaching the gospel and leading people to faith in Christ.

Several years ago I read a fascinating book titled *Protestants in Russia*. It told the story of Czar Alexander II, one of the infamous rulers of Russia in the early 1800s. He possessed absolute power (*Czar* is the Russian translation of *Caesar*) as well as unlimited wealth and a massive army to do his bidding.

Alexander II appeared to have it all. Wealth. Power. Absolute control. Then one day a distant cousin from Austria paid him a visit. Surveying his ostentatious palace, his numerous servants who catered to his every whim, and the opulent lifestyle he took for granted, she said, "You lack only one thing."

"What's that?" he replied, miffed that anyone could point out an inadequacy in his magisterial possessions.

"Jesus Christ," the baroness calmly replied. She went on to explain his need for a personal Savior.

If he was convicted by her comment, he didn't let on. He continued to amass wealth and expand his influence over the millions of subjects who owed him their complete subservience.

Then came an event that Alexander could have never foreseen. A short, determined general by the name of Napoleon decided that Russia should belong to him. His swarming French armies invaded Russia and drove the Czar's forces back as far as Moscow. Alexander II watched in horror as the city of Moscow burned before his very eyes. All that he had lived for, all the power and wealth and status that had consumed his every waking hour, was engulfed in a swirling column of smoke and flames. Observers say the incident left him deeply shaken. It was a spiritual turning point in his life.

With the cruel Russian winter as his ally, the Czar was able to rally his forces and launch a counteroffensive that drove Napoleon back in a bloody retreat across the frozen steppes of his empire. When Alexander returned victorious from his campaign, he went for a retreat in the Crimea. You can imagine the shock and disbelief of the Russian people when they learned their conquering hero had suddenly died in the Crimean peninsula. His coffin was returned to St. Petersburg for a state burial, but it was never opened.

At the same time a man by the name of Feodor appeared in the far eastern region of Siberia. A person of glowing faith, he spent the remainder of his life performing acts of mercy and kindness to the elderly and children. When he died, the people considered him a saint.

In 1933 the Communist government in Moscow ordered that all the coffins of the former Czars be opened to search for state jewelry and treasures. When they opened Czar Alexander II's casket, they were dumbfounded—it was empty. Some speculate that Alexander II, recognizing the futility and transitory nature of power and wealth, quietly gave up his throne to become Feodor, the man of compassion and faith in Siberia.

If that is indeed what happened, it is a lesson to us all. The kingdoms of this world, and the power, prestige, and possessions we so hotly pursue and contest, are insignificant when compared to the eternal value of the kingdom of our God, and of his Christ.

Our focus in the local church must remain on doing the work of Christ while we still have an opportunity. Jesus gave us a short and succinct job description: "Therefore go and make disciples of all nations, baptizing them in the name of the Father and of the Son and of the Holy Spirit" (Matt. 28:19). I agree with the bumper sticker that reads, "The main thing is to keep the main thing the main thing." Or as the apostle Paul said, to build unity and maintain right priorities, avoid the irrelevant.

Commit Random and Senseless Acts of Reconciliation

There are few things which dissolve anger and hardened attitudes in another person as effectively as kindness. Performing an act of grace and unselfishness toward a person we don't like can transform an enemy into a friend.

There was no more bitter or divisive conflict in American history than the Civil War. Yet on the day Abraham Lincoln heard that General Robert E. Lee had surrendered his army at Appomattox Courthouse, he walked outside the White House and instructed the U.S. Marine Corps band to play "Dixie."

It is often a single gesture or act of kindness that can begin the healing of wounds and disunity within a congregation. Pastors can, by a single sincere act of love and concern for an opponent, change the atmosphere of a church from one of acrimony to acceptance.

I recall a time when I moved too quickly on an idea, and it led to considerable disruption. I was serving an inner-city church that was looking to increase its outreach to the community. We wanted to begin a Sunday service and lunch for the unchurched, but our building seemed inadequate. Our clothes and food distribution ministry had expanded to the point where some Sundays, groceries and clothing were stacked on the front pews.

There was a rather large and modern church facility across the street from us that had recently built an addition. It was newer, more attractive, and had considerable space. I suggested we rent their facility on Sunday afternoons to hold our outreach service and meal. In my enthusiasm, I approached their pastor about the idea and he was open to it. A sister church of ours even offered to underwrite the rent. I was ecstatic.

But not everyone in the congregation shared my enthusiasm. A number of people, particularly a sizable group of older members, objected to the plan. The other church was of a different denomination than we were. There was also the fear we would lose our identity as a church if we held our services in another building. Where I saw the move as the dawn of a new day for our ministry, others saw it as a one-way trip down Sunset Boulevard.

The dissension in the church came out into the open. The atmosphere on the Sunday morning before we were to take the vote was heavier than a crate of hymnals on Saturn. By the evening meeting, it was clear the opposition was not only digging in their heels, they were wearing cement shoes. They produced a petition signed by a number of individuals who opposed the move to the other building. In fairness, they did propose a compromise. If we would hold our regular Sunday morning worship service in our building, then we could hold the outreach service and meal at the other.

As the moment of the vote arrived, I remember looking at the group opposed to the plan and thinking, "These people are not my opponents. They are members of the flock I'm supposed to shepherd."

Though I suspected there were enough votes on my side to pass my proposal, I changed my mind. I rose and said, "I am your pastor, and we are one congregation. I do not feel comfortable adopting this measure by a 55 percent to 45 percent margin. I suggest we table it until we can reach a true consensus. I don't want to go ahead with this unless we can go ahead as a united church."

I wish you could have seen the expressions on the faces of the opposition. They were stunned. None of them had expected me to back down. But in my heart, I knew it was the right thing to do. Though I had great dreams for what we could do as a church, they could not be accomplished with a severed body. The unity of the church had to take priority.

A few months later, when we proposed an afternoon service for community residents that would include a free lunch in our basement, it passed unanimously. People who had been dead-set against the original plan got behind this proposal in a big way. Most showed up for our first service.

Within just a few weeks we had a hundred people and more

sharing a meal together each Sunday. It launched a new day in the church's ministry and sense of unity. Nearly a decade later, that program continues.

Someone has said, "When in doubt, choose kindness." In this case, kindness meant setting aside my agenda and listening to the needs and concerns of an opposing group. It was a random and senseless act of reconciliation that opened the door to genuine unity and purpose.

Paul tells pastors they "must be kind to everyone" (2 Tim. 2:24). In a world that values power, dominance, and winning at all costs, there is little room left for an act of tenderness, particularly toward one's opponents. But that is the way of unity.

A president was once sent a letter requesting a pardon. There were no accompanying letters of recommendation.

"What? Has this man no friends?" asked the president.

"Apparently not, sir," replied the aide.

"Then I shall be his friend," said the president, and he signed the pardon.

Unity and harmony occur when we treat our enemies just as we treat our friends, and commit an occasional random and senseless act of reconciliation toward them.

Breaking Bones with Gentleness

Pastors are natural targets for criticism. Consider these two letters that Ed Dobson, pastor of Calvary Church in Grand Rapids, Michigan, received the week after Easter Sunday:

Dear Pastor Dobson,

This was [written] after considerable prayer. My husband and I are submitting to the will of God and the urging of other saints by walking away from your church.

While we could easily slip out unnoticed and certainly never be missed, which is definitely one of the problems here, I feel that our reasons for leaving are important enough to share with you.

Our church in one broad sweep is trampling the grace of God and mocking the Gospel. The church is the body of Christ, Pastor Dobson, not the unsaved masses of humanity you're trying to attract. Our church offers a program for every aspect of society that sets its foot in its walls—single moms, single dads, fatherless children, divorced women, substance abusers, but virtually nothing for believers.

Although the church may be growing, you are losing the true saints of God. If this has been your goal, you are to be congratulated because you're achieving it. If not, there's still time to turn away.

In Christ, a saint.

P.S. "And thou, Capernaum, which art exalted unto heaven, shalt be brought down to hell: for if the mighty works, which have been done in thee, had been done in Sodom, it would have remained until this day. But I say unto you, That it shall be more tolerable for the land of Sodom in the day of judgment, than for thee."

That week he received another letter in response to his Easter sermon titled, "Smile, It's Easter and God Loves You." The letter read in part,

Greetings.

Visits to your church have left the following impressions.... [There was] a vapid, soft, and comfortable presentation on Easter with the emphasis on smile rather than our sinfulness driving the Suffering Servant to the Cross. This was so irreverent and out of place as to make one ashamed, not of the Gospel, but of its hapless, harmless, one-sided view...God help us. Whatever happened to the offense of the Cross?

An Unhappy Camper.[8]

While it is impossible to respond to unsigned letters, Ed Dobson through the years has made it his practice to call each person who writes and signs a letter of criticism. His purpose is not to counterattack or defend himself, but to be certain he understands their concerns and they understand his position. Dobson explains why he deliberately adopted a strategy of gentleness in dealing with harsh critics:

When I was younger, I resisted bearing criticism. Rather than using my call as a pillar to lean on during times of criticism, I used it as a baseball bat to challenge my critics head-on.

Part of that was due to my training. It had been drilled into me during college that regardless of the cost, you have to take a stand. If the whole world is against you, take a stand. So during my first pastorate, I interpreted that to mean I should stand up to my critics.

When I would encounter conflict in the board meetings, I would bring up the issue in my sermon the next Sunday.

"God called me to start this church," I would remind the congregation. "If you don't like it, there are a number of other churches in this town you can attend." I declared the authority of the pastor and expected that to end the issue.

As I look back, that was really a stupid thing to do.

While we ought to stand for what we believe, Paul says we are to teach and admonish others in a spirit of patience and gentleness. Hopefully I've grown in this regard.

Today, when I encounter tough opposition or a stinging criticism, I ask myself, "Is God trying to show me something in this? Is this a process of character development in my own life?"[9]

The writer of Proverbs tells us, "Through patience a ruler can be persuaded, and a gentle tongue can break a bone" (Prov. 25:15). Gentleness can accomplish far more than brute strength or relentless aggression can ever achieve.

My daughter has always wanted a cat. It is not her nature to argue or beg. But she is persistent. She began by bringing home posters of kittens.

"See these Dad?" she would say.

"You can't have one, darling," I would reply.

"Okay." And she would drop the matter.

Then when it was time to order books from school, she would show me her selection. They were all stories of cats.

"Your mother and I have decided no cats," I would say.

"All right, Dad," she would say with a smile. Nothing more was said.

Then came Christmas. We asked each child to make a short list of gifts they wanted. When we picked up her list, every item was the same thing: "I want a cat."

"We've already talked about this; no cat," I would say.

"Whatever you say, Father," she would reply.

I don't need to tell you her campaign of patience and gentleness was beginning to wear us down. I came to my desk one day to find Post-it notes all over the room. They all had cat paw prints drawn on them.

147

Not long after, we as a family crowded into a small room in a local animal shelter to select a cat. As I walked down the aisle of the supermarket and dropped a box of Tender Vittles in the shopping cart, I knew I had been beaten. By an eight-year-old. Who happened to have patience.

Anyone can get angry. It takes no special talent to lose your temper and get mean. I know, I've done it. Ugly and threatening exchanges are not hard to come by in our world. But a gentle answer is hard to find, and is the sure mark of a mature and growing believer.

People rarely escalate their anger and criticism toward a pastor who responds in gentleness and patience. It does happen, but more often gentleness has a way of disarming our critics and opponents. The writer of Proverbs observes, "A gentle answer turns away wrath, but a harsh word stirs up anger" (Prov. 15:1).

Remember, the person who is in control of his responses is ultimately in control of the situation. Gentleness and patience are not signs of weakness, but of maturity and strength. They are vital components of unity.

People who tend to rise in corporate and business structures (and stay up there) are not the bullies and the intimidators. These people eventually self-destruct. Most leaders who endure are men and women who know how to control their tempers and give gracious answers despite the provocations they receive. Pastors who can restrain their anger and deal with criticism honestly but graciously will likely outlast and outlive their opponents. They will also help create a climate of unity and harmony.

Liberate, Don't Eliminate

A final and vital step a pastor can take to promote unity in the local church is to pray for, not punish, critics and opponents. We ought to sincerely pray for our critics to see God's truth in a clear and liberating fashion. Paul puts it this way, "Those who oppose [the Lord's servant] he must gently instruct, in the hope

that God will grant them repentance leading them to a knowledge of the truth, and that they will come to their senses and
escape the trap of the devil, who has taken them captive to do
his will" (2 Tim. 2:25-26).

Few antagonists in the church are aware that their ungodly
behavior or divisive actions may be serving an evil purpose. They
often sincerely believe they're doing what they're doing for the
good of everyone.

But that's the way deception works. If we knew we were
being deceived, we would probably change course. But deception
is subtle, seductive, and usually has the appearance of good. As
Paul reminds us, "for Satan himself masquerades as an angel of
light" (2 Cor. 11:14).

But when deception enters our lives, we end up caught in a
trap. Because we are believing a lie, we end up living a lie.
Ultimately, we end up doing the will of the devil rather than the
will of God.

How should we respond to those who are deceived in this
way?

Our natural instinct is to try to get rid of our enemies. The
Pharisees certainly thought they were doing God a favor when
they had Jesus arrested and eventually put to death. The
Crusaders thought they were doing God a favor when they slew
the occupants of Jerusalem during the Middle Ages. And the officials who had the Anabaptists drowned during the Reformation
era probably thought they too were doing God a favor.

Often when we do pray for our critics in the local church, we
pray that they will simply leave. That may be prudent in some
cases, but God's first priority is to ask that they might come to a
knowledge of the truth.

One of the most stinging phone calls I ever received came
from a woman whose wedding I would not perform. Some weeks
earlier she and her fiancé had called the church asking to be

married there. I met with them and said, "Bill and Brenda, I'll agree to meet with you for several sessions. But I won't promise to marry you two. I'll make that decision after I've gotten to know the both of you better."

They both agreed. After several weeks of counseling with them, I became uneasy. Something was wrong in their relationship. I couldn't quite pinpoint it, but something wasn't right. I wrestled with my decision, then finally admitted to myself I couldn't go through with it.

One afternoon Brenda called to finalize the arrangements for the wedding. "Pastor," she began, "I think it's important we nail down a date now. How about—"

"Brenda, excuse me for breaking in," I replied. "But I have had to make a very difficult decision."

"What?" she said in a concerned voice.

"I'm afraid I can't marry you and Bill. I don't believe he loves you. I don't think he wants to get married."

"You won't what?" she yelled into the phone. She then let me have it. If memory serves me correctly, she went on to describe my character in less than glowing terms. "Well then, I'll just find a pastor who's a real pastor. Not someone like you." She slammed down the phone.

I didn't hear again from Brenda for several weeks, not until the Sunday I spotted her in the front pew. She smiled at me and seemed so much more peaceful.

She walked through the greeting line at the end of the service and extended her hand, "Pastor, do you remember me?"

"Why, of course, Brenda," I said. (How could I forget?) "What's happened since we last talked?"

"You remember how you told me that Bill didn't love me?" she said. "Well, I called him that same day and told him what you had said."

"And?"

"And he said you were right," she replied. "He said he didn't love me and he didn't want to get married. So we called off the wedding."

Later I learned that Brenda had suffered a miscarriage before she and her fiancé had come for counseling. She had deceived herself into believing she and Bill were in love and were right for each other. And they had tried to deceive me about the nature of their relationship.

I'm glad I chose the road of gentle instruction and that God granted her a knowledge of the truth. She was not my enemy because she yelled at me, she was a victim of a deception she eventually recognized.

We live in a culture in which deceptions of all sort abound. Perhaps the most common deception in the church is the idea that the church belongs to us. It doesn't.

Virtually every church consultant I interviewed or studied in preparation for this book agreed on one frequent source of conflict: people who feel they own the church. Often it is those who have been there the longest who feel that way. Conflict erupts when they perceive they are losing control of "their church." It doesn't matter what the issue might be, whether it's a style of music or dropping the Sunday evening service—when one group senses it's losing control to another, conflict begins.

But that's where good theology can save us from disunity and disharmony. Biblical theology teaches us that the church belongs to Jesus Christ, the Head, the Lord of his people. Neither the pastor, nor the board, nor the original stake-holders can claim the church belongs to them. Remember Paul's words, "And God placed all things under his feet and appointed him to be head over everything for the church, which is his body, the fullness of him who fills everything in every way" (Eph. 1:22-23).

Those who insist on trying to maintain ownership of a local church as if it's a hamburger franchise are guilty of rebellion. It's not their church, it's not the pastor's church, it's Christ's church. If they continue to insist it belongs to them, and are successful in seizing and maintaining control, they will probably live to see their church's demise.

Churches that live in the glow of yesterday's accomplishments and yesterday's pastors, but refuse to allow new leaders and new visions to enter in, will ultimately see their church decline. People grow old and die. When one generation passes on without handing the mantle of leadership to another, you end up like the Shakers in Kentucky. They didn't believe in sexual relationships in marriage, so by the twentieth century, they were down to two people. No reproduction, no one to carry on, eventually no church.

The same is true of pastors who are reluctant to leave or turn over the mantle of leadership to another. It's particularly a temptation when a pastor has enjoyed a long and prosperous tenure. They just can't let go.

Pastor John had been at the same church for twenty-five years. When he retired from that church, he left reluctantly. He sent subtle signals that if the people really loved him, they would reject his successor and all those who tried to follow him.

The leadership picked up on his subconscious cues, and sure enough, they ran off everyone who tried to fill his shoes. The church steadily declined. All the good that Pastor John did during his tenure was eventually undone by his unwillingness to let go of the church. Both pastors and lay people must yield control of the church to its rightful Lord and Master if unity is to prevail.

We can only pray for those are deceived, whether they be pastors or lay people, that God will grant them repentance and a knowledge of the truth. But it is prayer, not pressure to leave, that God uses to change hearts. Our prayer purpose should be to liberate, not eliminate.

Put Love into Action

It's important that a church not maintain simply a reactive mode to conflict. Churches need to take positive steps to prevent conflict from occurring. John Sheaffer, a pastor in the midwest, recommends four practical steps any church can take to help promote a spirit of harmony and unity in the congregation:

1. Once a year take a written survey of your congregation.

This type of survey allows people to express their concerns about various programs or aspects of church life. They don't have to sign their names if they don't wish to. The staff and official board then study the results to determine what's working well and where the trouble spots might lie that need their attention.

2. Once a year do a phone survey of your congregation.

The staff and board members divide up the list and call each member and active participant in the congregation. The survey is intended to help the leadership listen to the needs and concerns of people. It also offers the advantage of follow-up questions to determine just what the person is saying. These results are also presented to the board for discussion and action as needed.

3. Pray for unity on a consistent basis.

The staff, board, and leadership of the church make it a matter of high priority to continually pray for the oneness of mind and heart of the congregation. While problems still arise, the spirit of prayer changes the atmosphere in which they are discussed and dealt with. They feel maintaining unity requires divine protection and assistance of God's presence in all the various aspects of the church's life.

4. Finally, stress a common vision.

"Kingdom people building kingdom families," is the unique vision of Pastor Sheaffer's church. Vision statements will always be as unique as the church itself, but it provides a common goal for the congregation to strive after. That, in and of itself, helps promote unity.

As most physicians will tell you, the best way to treat disease is to prevent it. In the same manner, the best way to deal with church conflict is to take active steps to stop it from ever getting started.

Conclusion

Pastors who respond with gentleness to difficult people and who pray for their opponents are a key to church unity. They send the message that this church is a safe place to be. It's mature enough to handle disagreements and its leadership is committed to building true community.

Bill Hybels is one such pastor. He describes how he works to deliberately face problems in a loving and accepting environment:

> Once a month I stand in front of the whole congregation and emcee an open question-and-answer time for half an hour. People can ask anything and everything—financial questions, personal questions, rumor questions. If people feel hesitant to ask a question publicly, they can submit it in writing before the session. I address every question.

> Recently, before one of the meetings, I reminded the congregation, "When you stand and ask your question, remember that pastors have feelings, too. So, if you're going to come after me, remember my heart is as fragile as your own."

> Sometimes, though, someone will ask a question that has an edge to it. When that happens I'll ask that person to pose the question again, in a more careful way. That process is a subtle way of training the church how to phrase disagreement so that no one is wounded and how to react when attacked.

And they're learning. Our congregation has developed the habit of hissing—when I tell a joke they don't think is funny or make a statement that they don't think is tactful. On occasion, they've even hissed a careless questioner. It's their lighthearted but firm way of saying, "That's not the way to fight fair."[10]

Peace and unity in a church don't just happen. They must be pursued, and the person to lead that pursuit is the pastor. Pastors must both model and train their congregations in the ways of building harmony.

As one pastor said to me, "When you treat people with grace and acceptance, you're training them how to treat you."

Notes
1. "Standing in the Crossfire: An Interview with Bill Hybels," *Leadership Journal* 14 (Winter 1993):20-21.
2. Ibid., 14.
3. H. B. London, "Resolving Conflict: Tearing Down the Walls that Separate," *Pastor to Pastor Newsletter*, February 1994, 1.
4. Personal interview with Ben Patterson.
5. Ibid.
6. Michelle Prentice-Leslie, "Good Grief and Holy Cow," *Leadership Journal* 14 (Summer 1993):72.
7. "Standing in the Crossfire," 18-19.
8. Personal interview with Edward G. Dobson.
9. Ibid.
10. "Standing in the Crossfire," 16.

A Tale of Two Parishes

How a pastor or board member responds to a conflict is often more important than the issue itself. If a pastor or leader deals with it individually, Lone Ranger style, it can easily degenerate into a one-on-one personality conflict. But if the problem is dealt with by a group, operating according to established guidelines and standards, the prospect for successful resolution is much higher. The choice we make in such situations can make all the difference in the world.

Scenario One

"Pastor, please pardon the interruption, but you need to take this call," said the female voice over the intercom.

"Jean, this is my study time. I have to prepare for the Oldheim funeral and I only have two hours left," said Pastor Young. The young pastor in his early thirties was really sweating this one. The members of Stella Oldheim's family were all unchurched people, and the elderly woman's final request at the hospital had been, "Pastor, preach the best sermon of your life at my funeral. Not for my sake, but for my relatives. It's the only chance I have to see any of them in heaven."

The weight of that deathbed request hung heavy around his neck.

"I'm sorry, Pastor," said the secretary. "But it's Fred Bostrom. He's on the other line and he's quite upset. He's says if I don't put him through to you right away, he's calling the elder board chairman."

Pastor Young put his head in his hands. *Why now?* "Okay, Jean, put him through." It seemed like it had been one headache after another ever since he had accepted the call to Trinity Church, a long-established church on the outskirts of Atlanta.

The light on his second phone line blinked green. He prayed quietly, "Lord, help me keep my calm with Fred." He reached over with reluctance and picked up the receiver. "Fred, how nice of you to call. What can I do for you?" he said in his best "parish" voice.

"No need for small talk, pastor. I'll get right to the point," snapped Fred. "It's about the music on Sunday morning. If we hear one more praise chorus, Bernice and I are leaving. We are sick and tired of trying to sing along with these new tunes we don't know and we don't like. No one our age knows them. What's wrong with the old hymns? I remember the days when we would sing through the gospel hymnbook twice a year. People got saved. You could hear the singing four blocks away. It was wonderful. Now, with guitars, drums, and all that other noise, it just doesn't seem like church anymore."

Pastor Young could feel his stomach tighten. Since the day he arrived at Trinity he had tried his best to get the church growing again. He had focused much of his effort on bringing in new couples. But that required a change in the worship format. So he had initiated a number of individual changes. For example, Young hadn't asked anyone except the elder chairman when he purchased new chorus books with money from his own pocket.

He had also contacted a young couple in the congregation to play contemporary music on Sundays.

The reactions to his changes had been swift and strong. The second week Ralph and Emily Barnes walked out of the service when an electric guitarist and tenor saxophonist played their rendition of "Amazing Grace."

"Pastor, are you there?" said Bostrom.

"Yes, Fred. I understand not everyone appreciates the new music. Change is hard."

"I'm not sure you do understand, pastor. People don't like what's happened. If you would just quit trying to make us sing this new music and let us have our hymnals back, everything would be fine. What's wrong with singing 'Love Lifted Me' this Sunday?' I remember it was Pastor Johansen's favorite hymn."

Pastor Johansen. That's all Pastor Young had heard about since he had arrived at the church. Johansen had been their pastor for nearly twenty years. When he retired two years ago, it was like a death in the family.

"Fred, please be patient," said the pastor. "There are a lot of people who like the music. We're keeping more and more of our visitors with the new format."

"That's another thing. Some of us are getting the feeling the only people you care about are newcomers. We're beginning to feel like used furniture."

Pastor Young bit his lip in anger. "What are you trying to say, Fred?"

"I think you're trying to get rid of us."

"That's not true; that's simply not true, Fred." Pastor Young could feel his blood pressure go up. "You're not giving me a chance."

"Pastor, I hesitate to say this to you, but someone needs to. You're ruining this church. If we don't get our music back, the music we grew up with, the music we were saved with, we're going to quit giving."

Pastor Young struggled to contain his anger, "Fred, that could almost be interpreted as a threat."

"It ain't no threat, it's for real. Why should we support a worship service that sounds like a jazz nightclub? I guarantee you, Pastor Johansen would never have caved in to worldliness the way you have."

"I take offense at that charge, Fred," said the pastor, his voice trembling. "Show me one single lyric that's been worldly, and I'll publicly apologize."

"Take it any way you wish, pastor. I've said my piece. Now you know how we feel. Goodbye." The phone clicked on the other end.

"And good day to you, too," said the pastor, slamming the phone down hard. He wheeled around in his chair and took a deep breath. He had to put aside Stella Oldheim's funeral message. He now had a church rebellion on his hands.

After a minute or two, he regained his calm. He decided to call Jim Stearns, the church chairman. A business executive in his midfifties, Jim was an amiable guy who tried hard to bridge the growing gap between old and young in the church. Pastor Young dialed the number and waited for an answer.

"Jim Stearns here," came the voice.

"Jim, sorry to bother you in the middle of the day."

"Pastor, is that you? Hey, can you hold on a second? I need to bring a conversation in my office to an end. I'll be back to you in two minutes."

The delay irritated Pastor Young but he had no choice. While he was put on hold, he replayed the conversation with Fred Bostrom over and over again. *Imagine the gall, to call up and try and blackmail me that way. Next time he calls, I'll be ready for him.* The light classical music on the phone quit when Jim came back on the line.

"What can I do for you, pastor?"

"I just got a call from Fred Bostrom. In the space of five minutes he threatened to leave the church, stop tithing, and accused me of being worldly. All because of the praise choruses and contemporary band we use."

Young could hear Stearns chuckling on the other end of the line.

"What are you laughing about, Jim? This is serious."

"Oh, you need to know Fred. He was just letting off some steam. He does that every now and then. Don't take him seriously, Ed."

"Well I don't care for his steam, Jim. I'm the one who got scalded."

"I'm sorry, Ed. I didn't mean to make light of what he said. But you can't take Fred all that seriously. Just let it go for now. Sure, I've heard some grumbling over the music, but there will always be some of that when you try something new. Almost everyone is behind you."

"I think it's more serious than you realize, Jim. I think there's a group out there opposed to me being here."

"Go on, Ed. The vote was almost unanimous to call you. Hey, I'll tell you what. Why don't you pay Fred and Bernice a visit? Have coffee with them. Bring them some Danish. That's all they want."

"You're making this sound like it's all my problem, Jim, and it's not. You know this church needed to update its music. Who in the world are we ever going to attract if we keep singing, 'Throw Out the Life Line'?"

"I know, I know. But just humor Fred and Bernice. Hey, go over to their house, look at the pictures of the grandchildren, let them show you slides of their trip to the Holy Land. Everything will be fine. I guarantee you."

"Jim, I think this thing is going to blow if we don't deal with it. But I'm not backing down. No sir. I'm willing to risk my job on the music. If that doesn't go the right direction, there's no use in me being here."

"Now calm down, Ed. It isn't all that bad. We can talk about it next month at the elder meeting. But for now, just humor Fred. Can't we sing something like, 'Heaven Came Down' this Sunday? It would be a good peace gesture."

"The music is already set for Sunday, Jim. It wouldn't be fair to the musicians to change it now. Besides, if we sing that stuff, half of the new families are going to get up and leave."

"Okay, pastor. Hey, I have someone else in my office. Gotta go. Talk to you later."

Pastor Young was still angry when he hung up. *My own board chairman doesn't take me seriously.* He glanced at the clock. *Oh, no.* It was now 11:50 A.M. and he still wasn't done with his sermon. He had to be at the funeral home at 12:30.

Pastor Young jotted down a few more notes, then yanked his suit coat on. He stopped to straighten his tie, then ran out the door. He made it to the funeral home just minutes before the crowds started to arrive.

Despite the unsettling phone call, he still managed to preach a good sermon. But as he drove away from the hilly, green cemetery after the interment, his thoughts went back to Fred.

What if there is something to his threats? What if he truly has a following? Home visit. Yeah, right. What chance would there be they could agree on anything. Besides, I'm not giving in on this issue. No way.

The next Sunday the congregation looked slightly smaller. When the overhead projector went on and the lyrics to the chorus appeared on the screen, he saw several scowls around the auditorium. He chose to ignore them. Besides, the newcomers sang loudly and with feeling.

As Young stood to shake hands with people after the service, he noticed that several of the older people who usually stopped to greet him went out the other door.

A month later it was time for the quarterly business meeting. For the last week, the disgruntled members had been unusually quiet. There was nothing spectacular on the agenda, just a proposal to seal the parking lot and have repairs done on the church van. Giving was down, but that was usual for this time of year.

Jim Stearns, the moderator, was good natured as usual. Most items passed with little or no discussion. The last item before adjournment was "New Business." It looked like everyone was going to get to go home early.

"Is there anything else we should talk about this evening?" Jim asked as he reached for a glass of water. "If not, we can entertain a motion to close the meeting and go home."

"I'd like to say something, Jim." The two hundred or so people who were there all turned their heads. Fred Bostrom, dressed in a light blue leisure suit, stood up to speak. His face appeared red and tense, a hint of sweat on his forehead. He stood so suddenly that he knocked over the folding chair in front of him. A loud clank resonated through the gymnasium.

"Sure, Fred, what's on your mind?" Jim said.

Pastor Young felt a wave of anxiety sweep over him. *Oh, terrific. Here it comes.*

Though arthritis had slowed his gait, Fred walked with obvious determination up the middle aisle to the microphone. His wife looked worried. Others in the back strained to hear what he was going to say. His voice faltered as he held up a statement he had written out to read for the group.

"Mr. Chairman, we, the people of Trinity Church, believe worship should be conducted in 'decency and order,' as the apostle Paul commands. Furthermore, we believe we are 'to come out and be separate from the world,' not feeding on the appetites of the flesh and the carnal mind. Sadly to say, our current pastor, Reverend Young, apparently does not wish to heed the Scriptures in these regards. The changes he has introduced into our once peaceful and happy church are worldly and of the flesh. He has been rebuked accordingly but has chosen to turn a deaf ear to the Scriptures."

Ed had trouble staying seated. His wife held his hand and pulled him back down.

"After much prayer and soul-searching, we the undersigned call for his resignation immediately. We believe the board should give Pastor Young three months severance pay to help him find a church more suited to his beliefs. Furthermore, we believe that our old hymn books should be put back in the pews as of this Sunday and worldly instruments no longer be allowed to dese-crate our worship."

Fred put down his paper and looked at the stunned minister, "Pastor Young, I'm sorry it had to come to this. But this is God's church, and we can't allow you to ruin it." Ed felt all the blood drain from his face.

"I second that motion!" came a loud voice from the back of the gymnasium. Harold Oberstar stood and waved his hand toward the moderator. "I second Fred's motion."

"Fred, come on, you can't be serious," Jim said in an easy-going voice. "I know you have some concerns about the worship service, but surely you can't mean—"

"I mean every word of what I said," he thundered. "You might as well all know the truth. I have here twenty-five signa-tures on this petition. More called the house, but weren't able to get here for tonight's meeting. Like Freida Ingersoll—you all know Freida—she's terribly upset by what's happening at Trinity."

"But she's been in a nursing home for seven years," Pastor Young whispered to his wife. "She's never even been to a worship service here."

"Mr. Chairman, I strongly object to what's happening tonight," came a voice from the second row. Dave Greer, one of the newcomers to the church, stood up. "How dare we consider firing Pastor Young? I think we all owe the pastor an apology."

"You go find your own church if you want night club music," said Fred in an angry voice.

"You're way out of line, Fred," said another board member, who now also stood to Ed's defense.

"Neither of you were here when we dug out the trees on this property to build this gymnasium. You're forgetting who the people are who made this church what it is. Who sacrificed to build it. We're taking back what rightly belongs to us. As for you, young man, you have a few things to learn."

"Gentlemen, gentlemen, please," Jim said. "This is not the place to discuss these issues. Why don't we all adjourn, go home for the night, and cool off a little."

"It's time we face the truth," shouted someone in the back. "We made a mistake when we called Pastor Young. He's not the right man for us."

Pastor Young's wife started to cry, and she got up and walked out. A younger woman followed her out the door.

"You can't talk about my pastor that way!" shouted Jerry Jansen, a strong supporter of Ed Young.

"Who are you to talk?" shouted another. "We all know you went bankrupt four years ago."

Several of the newer converts in the church sat in stunned silence. They had no idea Christians could talk this way to each other.

"People, people, please," pleaded the moderator. But the meeting had gotten out of his control. Several older members were now on their feet shouting at several younger members who were also on their feet.

"If the pastor goes, we go with him," said one middle-aged man. His three elementary and junior high-aged children just sat there, frightened looks on their faces.

"And if he stays, we go," shouted one of Fred Bostrom's supporters.

Pastor Young couldn't take any more of this. He picked up his agenda, crumpled it in his hands, and walked out a side door. His wife stood outside the door, her eyes red and swollen.

"Pastor, please come back. Don't go," he heard someone yell behind him. He ignored their voice and stormed out into the parking lot. He opened the door for his wife, got in behind the wheel, cranked the engine over, and sped out of the lot.

Three days later, his resignation arrived in the mail at Jim Stearn's office. Two weeks later, the congregation was half its size.

Two years later, Trinity was still without a pastor.

Scenario Two

The light on Ed Young's second phone line blinked green. He prayed quietly, "Lord, help me keep my calm with Fred." He reached over with reluctance and picked up the receiver. "Fred, how nice of you to call. What can I do for you?" he said in his best "parish" voice.

"No need for small talk, pastor. I'll get right to the point," snapped Fred. "It's about the music on Sunday morning. If we hear one more praise chorus, Bernice and I are leaving. What's wrong with the old hymns? I remember the days when we would sing through the gospel hymn book twice a year. It was wonderful. Now, with guitars, drums, and all that other noise, it just doesn't seem like church anymore."

"I understand not everyone appreciates the new music, Fred. Change is hard."

"I'm not sure you do understand, pastor" Fred replied. "People don't like what's happened. If you would just quit trying to make us sing this new music and let us have our hymnals back everything would be fine."

"Fred, please be patient. There are a lot of people who like the music. We are keeping more and more of our visitors with the new format."

"That's another thing. Some of us are getting the feeling the only people you care about are newcomers. We're beginning to feel like used furniture."

Pastor Young was tempted to respond to Fred's statement as a personal attack, but thought better of it. He was not going to deal with an issue of this magnitude on his own. He decided to try to hear Fred out. At least that way he'd have accurate information to share with the appropriate committee.

"Fred, it sounds like you and others have some very deep concerns. Concerns that we need to be sensitive to as a board and staff."

There was a long silence on the other end.

"Well, thank you, pastor," Fred sounded a bit off balance. "To be truthful, that's not the response I thought I'd get from you."

"Fred, I'm your pastor. I'm pastor to all the people of Trinity Church. While I want to see us grow and reach out, I also want you and the others who have been here much longer than I to be a part of that effort."

There was another moment of awkward silence.

"Well...I appreciate you listening, pastor. I really do. It's hard to get older and see so much of what's familiar slip away."

"Like Stella Oldheim?"

"Yes, Bernice and are going to miss her."

"Fred, let me make this promise to you. I'm going to be meeting with Jim Stearns for lunch tomorrow. Perhaps we have moved a little quickly on the music. This is an issue that demands careful consideration, not an off-the-cuff response from me or anyone else. I promise you a reply no later than Friday. Is that agreeable?"

"I...I guess so."

"Good. I'm sorry I have to run, but Stella's funeral starts in less than ninety minutes. Will I see you and Bernice there?"

"Yes, Stella was one of Bernice's bridesmaids. We all got married the same year." Pastor Young was beginning to realize just how much loss Fred was absorbing these days.

"Pray for me, will you Fred?"

"Sure thing, pastor. Let's pray right now."

When they were finished, Pastor Young hung up the phone and swung around toward the window. He mused for a minute or two then reached over and picked up the phone. He dialed the number of Jim Stearns, the board chairman. A business executive in his midfifties, Jim tried hard to bridge the growing gap between old and young in the church. Ed dialed the number and waited for an answer.

"Jim Stearns here."

"Jim, sorry to bother you in the middle of the day."

"Pastor, is that you? Hey, can you hold on a second? I need to bring a conversation in my office to an end. I'll be back to you in two minutes."

The delay didn't bother Pastor Young, he knew Jim was a busy man. While he was put on hold he replayed the conversation with Fred Bostrom over and over again. *I can't allow this to become a personal issue between Fred and me. The leadership needs to face this as a group.*

Jim came back. "What can I do for you, pastor?"

"I just got a call from Fred Bostrom. He and his wife are quite upset with the worship changes we've made lately."

"I've heard similar rumblings, pastor. It was on my list of agenda items for our next executive meeting."

"Let me make a suggestion," said Pastor Young. "I think we made an error when we introduced the praise choruses and band without working through our theology of worship. This shouldn't be just my decision. The church and the leadership all need to own this."

"What are you suggesting?"

"Let's start over as an elder board with a study of worship from a scriptural point of view. It may take weeks, even months, but we need to have a firm biblical basis for what we do on Sunday mornings."

"We could invite input from Fred's age group," suggested Jim. "They need to know they're being heard."

"Precisely. My management theory instructor in college used to drill into us, 'Create a system to deal with conflict. Don't deal with it alone. Otherwise, it becomes personalized. Bring the resources of the entire group to bear on the problem. Remember, people tend to support solutions they helped to create.'"

"I like it, pastor. What do we do in the meantime?"

"Let's meet as elders this Thursday morning for breakfast. Let's examine some ways to meet the worship needs of Fred's group. We can prepare a statement I can read on Sunday. We'll announce the worship study and share a timetable for reporting back to the congregation."

"I'll call the other elders during my lunch break," said Jim.

"I have a funeral to go to," said Pastor Young.

"You don't want to be late for that."

"No pun intended, right Jim?"

"No, I assure you. I'll pray for you, pastor. Let's talk this over later this evening."

The elders met for breakfast that Thursday morning and crafted a carefully worded statement. It was agreed that Jim, rather than Pastor Young, should read it from the pulpit. This was to be a statement of the elders, not just the pastor.

The next Sunday morning, as the overhead projector went off, Pastor Young saw several scowls in the sanctuary, mainly from the older members. But they were his flock, and he was determined to love them. He stood up and smiled at the group.

"Friends and members, Jim Stearns, our elder chairman, has an important statement he'd like to read to you."

Jim walked up, shook hands with Pastor Young, then retrieved a statement from his coat pocket. He spread it out on the podium, then began to read:

"The worship of God is the most important thing we do. The Bible clearly says that God desires those who will worship him in spirit and in truth. The most important objective of worship is to glorify God. That requires that we worship in a spirit of unity and harmony, raising our hearts and voices as one to praise our Savior.

"Recently, we realized we may have made a mistake as an elder board. We implemented changes in our worship format without first giving careful study to what biblical worship is. We intend to correct that error. For the next three months, we will meet on Tuesday night an hour earlier than usual to consider what the Scripture has to say about proper worship."

There was a rumble of approval that came from the back of the sanctuary. Jim looked up over his half-glasses, then continued to read.

"We invite your input into this process. We are going to ask that the members of different ages and groups in the church meet with us to discuss their understanding of biblical worship. We guarantee everyone will be given a careful hearing. Please call the church secretary to arrange for a time slot to appear before the elder board once we reach that stage in the process. We'll give notice in the bulletin.

"Our goal is to arrive at a mission statement on worship that we can adopt as a congregation. We will then evaluate all our present practices and any further changes against that statement. We'll determine what fits our theology of worship and what does not."

Bernice poked her husband with her elbow. He smiled and turned around to say something to another couple that sat behind him.

The elder board was true to their word. For the next twelve weeks they met to study the Scriptures and discuss worship. After about eight weeks of study, they began inviting members of the congregation to the meeting to discuss their views.

There were times of difficulty. Occasionally emotions flared, but the openness of the board to everyone's concerns seemed to calm frayed nerves. They were able to come to a consensus on many issues. When they could not, they chose to continue to study and discuss until they reached a breakthrough.

It took longer than anticipated, but at last the final statement was ready for the quarterly business meeting. The room was packed with members and interested individuals. The chairman announced an agenda slightly out of the ordinary for that meeting.

"After the statement on worship has been read, which has the full support of the elder board, the pastoral staff, and the church's executive committee, we will allow a time for discussion and interaction. Following that, we will vote on the matter.

"Regardless of the outcome of the vote, we will then celebrate communion as a body of believers. That will be a time for all of us to search our hearts, ask God to show us attitudes and actions that perhaps have grieved him, and where he might prompt us to do so, seek the forgiveness of other members of this body."

Jim opened a black vinyl folder that contained the elder board's statement on worship.

"After long hours of the study of Scripture, prayer, dialogue, and interaction with a variety of members on the subject of worship, we have arrived at the following principles that shall guide the worship at Trinity Church:

"1. Worship exists first and foremost to glorify God in the persons of the Father, Son, and Holy Spirit. Therefore let us always remember that we worship God for his sake, not to please ourselves.

"2. Worship includes both a private and corporate act of preaching the Word, private and group prayer, communal singing, reading Scripture, observation of the Lord's supper and baptism, public testimony and private meditation, to be done in a spirit of humility, confession, praise, repentance, surrender, and a commitment to obedience. True worship recognizes the full character of God, including his holiness, graciousness, mercy, justice, all-powerful, all-loving, all-knowing nature. God is seeking those who will worship him in spirit and in truth.

"3. Worship is a celebration of the unity of the Father, Son, and Holy Spirit that ought to be reflected in our unity as redeemed members of the Body of Christ. Divisiveness and strife are therefore antithetical to true worship.

"4. Though we are many members, we are one body; though we are one body, we are many members. It is natural and acceptable that different styles and methods of worship may be preferred by some and not by others. Therefore we will seek to honor and incorporate a diversity of styles and elements of worship; we are always to prefer others before ourselves in love.

"5. Finally, we shall establish a worship commission, with members of the board, pastoral staff, and elected members of the church at large to supervise, evaluate, and modify our practice of worship to reflect the needs of the congregation as a whole. Concerns and suggestions are to be made directly to this group, acting on the biblical principle that we are to speak the truth in love to one another and to guard the unity of the Spirit in the bond of peace."

"That's it, folks, are there any questions?" Jim asked as he looked up from his podium.

"I have one," came a voice from the back row. It was Fred Bostrom. "Are we going to get our hymns back?"

"May I answer that?" Pastor Young asked.

"Be my guest," Jim said.

Pastor Young turned around and smiled at Fred. "Fred, I have an apology to make. I was so eager to expand the ministry of this church to others that I temporarily lost sight of your needs and the needs of others here. Worse yet, I may have left the impression that I love the one lost sheep more than I do the ninety-nine. Well I don't. I love all of you."

Fred nodded, an awkward smile on his face.

"So, Fred, before we vote on this issue, let me assure you that the music that has ministered to you through the years still has a place in this church. How we achieve a balance in new and traditional music is still for the worship commission to decide. But yes, we need to raise our children with an appreciation for traditional as well as contemporary music in the church."

Applause broke out in the back half of the room.

"I want to say one other thing Fred. Do you forgive me?" asked Pastor Young. Now all heads turned to see what Fred's response would be.

"Uh, pastor..." Fred cleared his throat. He seemed to struggle for his words. "I must confess that I...well, yes, I do." He looked down at his wife, Bernice, who was dabbing her eyes. "We want you to know that we love you, too. And we're sorry for the things we've said—I've said—to others about you. You are a wonderful shepherd."

Pastor Young stepped out of his row of chairs and made his way to the center aisle. He motioned for Fred to come toward him. Fred, who was raised in a home that found physical expressions of love awkward, scratched his ear and looked around.

"Go ahead, dear," his wife urged. "He won't hurt you."

Several of his older friends chuckled. Many of the younger families strained to see what Fred would do.

Finally, Fred started out of his row. His arthritis slowed him down, but he made his way to the center aisle, walked up to the pastor, and offered his hand. Pastor Young took it, then pulled Fred toward him and the two embraced.

The room broke into applause. Pastor Young turned toward

the pianist who was seated on the second row. "Ellen, would you mind getting up and playing one of my favorites, 'How Great Thou Art'?"

"Of course," she smiled. She got up and made her way over to the piano.

"No, Ellen," said Fred. Everyone looked his direction. "Please, let's sing...what do you call it? Oh, yes, 'Lamb of God.' Isn't that the name of that chorus, pastor?"

Pastor Young hugged Fred one more time.

That night the congregation sang both songs.

Pastor Young stayed there ten more years.

CHAPTER 8

Getting It into Your System

As the two scenarios in the last chapter demonstrated, the future of a local church may depend on how the pastor and leadership respond to conflict in its early stages. When conflict is either ignored or personalized, it usually continues to escalate and becomes even more dangerous. But when the pastor and leadership listen to the concerns of others, and respond to the issue using a systems approach, the prospects for restoring unity are much brighter.

What is a "systems approach" to conflict management? It's a method of solving conflict using established committees, policies, and standards to deal with problems and issues as they arise.

As a young pastor, Norm Shawchuck discovered the value of establishing a system to deal with problems in the church:

I knew I was in trouble when a church officer introduced himself to me and said, "I will sign the checks, but don't ask for any information regarding contributions or giving records. No one has been able to untangle that mess." I was so preoccupied with getting established that I let his comment go without asking any further questions.

The problem hit home when the year-end reports came due. Our denomination required that we send in full financial and membership reports. I asked the appropriate officer to fill out the reports, which he did. I also happened to request that he give me a copy of the records to document the numbers we were sending in.

He agreed to produce the records, but kept stalling. He gave me the excuse that he was transferring the figures from his files to the church records. When I still didn't receive the documents, I called him and said, "Bill, I just can't wait any longer. You must bring me your records tomorrow without fail." The next day Bill walked in the door with grocery bags full of notes, envelopes, and assorted stubs.

I asked the two church secretaries to help Bill put the material in order. A few days later, they handed me the results of their efforts. The membership rolls contained people who had been dead for years. Several membership classes had never been recorded. I was handed a batch of envelopes that contained money from an offering we had taken—seven years ago.

It was impossible for me to arrive at an accurate membership count, or substantiate the amount of contributions given by any one person. I sat down with a number of key leaders and put the matter before them. I was surprised to learn they weren't surprised at all. They had known for years that our records were a mess, but no one wanted to confront Bill.[1]

Shawchuck solved the problem by establishing policies and a system of accountability for record keeping. Because this new approach required self-discipline and supervision, Bill ultimately chose to resign on his own. Shawchuck was spared the potentially divisive decision of firing Bill. The system dealt with Bill, keeping the problem from becoming a personal issue between him and the pastor.

Nothing Personal

Leith Anderson, a pastor and author of several best-selling books on the church, strongly believes in a systems approach to dealing with individuals in conflict situations.

> What is the best way to correct people? Confrontation? Isolation? Punishment? I don't want the process of accountability to degenerate into personal attack. I believe it's better to establish a system that assumes responsibility for dealing with individuals, rather than always leaving it to the pastor.
>
> I don't have the energy or the wisdom to deal with every person that needs correction. Pastors who try and assume all the responsibility suffer for it. Their energy-level drops while the blood pressure skyrockets.
>
> I prefer to correct people using established standards and organized systems, rather than force of personality or power plays.
>
> When I say that, people's first reaction is, "How can an impersonal system deal with personal problems?" It's a mistaken notion to believe that systems have to be by definition cold and uncaring. In reality, systems are comprised of people too. But standard operating procedures bring order and fairness to the way people deal with each other.[2]

Few situations are more difficult to confront than when a leader becomes involved in immoral behavior. But even in these difficult instances, a systems approach to conflict has its advantages:

> I once had to confront a prominent leader who announced he was leaving his wife for another woman in the church. I called him and said, "I need to talk with you about your decision." We met over a meal and talked it through. I expressed my deep concerns over his intended course of action. But I based my objections on a foundation of clearly understood principles and expectations. I wasn't just expressing my views, but the established biblical and board standards of the church.

> When he came on the board, he accepted those guidelines as standards he would submit to. So in our conversation I reminded him of that commitment he had made. He even acknowledged the guidelines were valid. It made a painful encounter much easier.

> It's only fair that our lay leaders know what's expected of them. That way when correction is needed, everyone's talking the same language. If someone is not meeting our clearly defined standards, I rarely have to say anything. The group pressure kicks in and addresses their problem. It's a form of positive adult peer pressure. It keeps me from always having to play the part of the "heavy."[3]

Anderson believes that for correction to occur properly, expectations need to be clearly spelled out. "A systems approach to correction can provide the safeguards of fairness, consistency, and objectivity," he says.

How can a systems approach to solving conflict bring unity and healing to a church? Let's examine each of the principles Anderson suggests and examine how they can be applied in the local church.

Communicate Your Great Expectations

Churches don't always do a good job of communicating. Consider this bulletin announcement that was intended to alert the people to a special missionary speaker: "Come hear Bertha Belch all the way from Africa." Those people who showed up expecting some type of trans-Atlantic gastronomic feat were treated instead to a slide presentation.

For a church to experience unity, there has to be clear communication of expectations of what's acceptable and what's not in various areas of church life.

It was a bright, snowy morning in a Canadian province when Pastor Stuart pulled out of the parking lot after services to go home. Two miles from church, a familiar vehicle pulled alongside on the highway. One of the men from the church, a single man from Vancouver, held out a green deposit bag with the morning offering in it.

"Hi ya, pastor!" he yelled over the rush of wind. "I sure hope I don't drop this on the way home." The man laughed and the car zoomed past. The pastor glanced at the deposit bag and nearly veered off the road.

Perhaps Pastor Stuart could have shown more of a sense of humor, but the incident did reveal a problem. After asking a few questions, it turned out the church had no established guidelines regarding how money would be counted, transported, or deposited in the bank. No one had ever communicated to the ushers any expectations about counting offerings. The lack of a good system, not the individuals themselves, was at the root of the problem. The board began a discussion of how morning offerings should be handled. They eventually adopted these guidelines:

(a) Two members of the board will be present when monies are counted and deposited.
(b) These individuals will both sign the deposit record.

(c) Monies will be taken directly to the bank for deposit after the service (and never kept at home for the night).

(d) A counting committee will pick up the monies on Monday morning from the overnight deposit box to verify the deposit.

Daylight Wasting Time?

To many, this approach may all seem a grand waste of effort. After all, either you trust people or you don't. But that's precisely the problem. The moment a question or conflict arises, you don't want the issue to become a matter of personal trust or character. It is far better to treat it as a matter of following prescribed guidelines. The first approach becomes intensely personal; the second is merely procedural.

Which would you rather face?

The purpose of a systems approach is not to create a maze of rules, regulations, and policies that strangles the church under the weight of a suffocating bureaucracy. It is to provide for fairness, accuracy, and objectivity.

The other option—to have little or no system at all to deal with conflict—is more dangerous. When pastors and leaders simply fly by the seat of their pants, they are in a flight pattern to crash and burn. When there are no clear and understood expectations to appeal to, it becomes a matter of one person's force of personality against another's.

It reminds me of the pick-up baseball games we played in our neighborhood when I was a kid. About a dozen of us would swarm out onto a vacant lot after supper to play baseball. Things would go well for the first fifteen minutes or so. Then, inevitably, someone would try something stupid, like stealing home while the other team was retrieving the ball from the swamp across the street.

"Wait a minute!" someone would shout. "There's no stealing bases in this game."

"Who said?"

"I said, that's who."

In a matter of seconds both benches would clear, and one team would stand across from the other, shouting that the other team was cheating.

"Check out the rule book," someone would yell.

"You check it out!" someone would shout back.

Of course, none of us had ever owned a rule book, much less read one. It quickly became a matter of who could shout the loudest or who looked the toughest or whose big brother was playing that day. It often would end with someone grabbing the one baseball we had and saying, "I'm going home."

The same thing happens in the local church. "Where there is no revelation, the people cast off restraint," Proverbs 29:18 says. One application might be, "Where there are no guidelines, the offering can get waved out the window and fifty dollar bills land on someone else's windshield."

One area of potential disaster each local church must face is the possibility of sexual abuse by a volunteer or member. Many insurance companies now require churches to establish guidelines for selecting and screening volunteers who will work with children or teenagers.

There are some who might find it offensive to fill out a questionnaire that asks, "Have you ever been convicted of a misdemeanor or felony for sexual misconduct?" But it's for their own protection, and the protection of the children and the congregation. All it takes is one reported case of suspected child abuse, and that church can quickly find itself besieged with lawsuits, unwanted publicity, and a church-wide schism.

Of course, guidelines and expectations alone won't prevent such abuses from occurring. Nor is it likely a perpetrator will answer the questionnaire honestly. But it does send a clear signal to potential victimizers that this church is serious about protecting its children. That may be enough to send them packing for a more vulnerable and unsuspecting congregation (which I pray they will never find).

The principle of establishing guidelines for the good of all applies to numerous other areas of church life. Whether it's music, building maintenance, teaching adult classes, or leading a youth group, a church needs to clearly communicate the expectations it has for people involved in each area.

Then if a problem arises, the pastor and the leadership can point to established standards as the objective measure of whether or not there's a problem. Because everyone understands what's expected of them, correcting a person runs a far less chance of degenerating into a personality conflict or private vendetta.

Doing It by the Book

But where should a church begin in an effort to establish wise, workable, and consistent guidelines for areas of church life that have the greatest potential to create conflict?

The answer, of course, is the Scriptures. Paul said to young Timothy, who was attempting to lead a congregation of his own, "All Scripture is God-breathed and is useful for teaching, rebuking, correcting and training in righteousness, so that the man of God may be thoroughly equipped for every good work" (2 Tim. 3:16-17).

God's Word is ultimately the only reliable standard to measure the conduct and character of members in the church. The purpose is not to scrutinize the faults and shortcomings of another person's life, but to prepare each person for every good work.

I'm glad that my personal physician spent years in school pouring over textbooks in anatomy, physiology, and chemistry. I'm relieved he wasn't offended by the idea of building his practice on the fundamental truths of medicine. Because he took years to fill his mind with knowledge and wisdom, I'm confident that when I come to him with strep throat, he will prescribe antibiotics rather than pouring Clorox 2 down my throat. Church workers should also take the time to be thoroughly grounded in the Word of God.

Only the timeless wisdom of the Scriptures is adequate to develop useful standards for ordering church life.

Jim Delafield was pastor of a church in Indiana that ran an aggressive summer program for rural young people. He hired numerous college students to work for the summer months. On a camping trip to the Atlantic Ocean, one of his older female staff members began showing a persistent interest in one of the teenage boys. She was in her twenties; he was only sixteen.

One night while the group camped out, Pastor Delafield awoke in the early morning hours and decided to check on the campers. He stumbled across the female staff member and the sixteen-year-old boy sleeping side by side in the same tent. Delafield woke the two up and forced them to move to separate parts of the camp.

The next morning he confronted the staff member. She claimed she had done nothing wrong. He ordered her to stay away from the boy for the remainder of the trip. Once they arrived back home, he brought the matter to the attention of the appropriate council and asked she be removed from the staff.

While she acknowledged the incident did occur, she claimed the right to stay on staff and receive her salary. In her eyes, they had done nothing more than help keep each other warm (a basic survival technique in the wilderness).

The church stood behind the pastor's actions. Why? First, the adult/minor age issue had clear legal implications. But more important, she had violated scriptural standards for behavior in the church. Ephesians 5:3 tells us, "But among you there must not be even a hint of sexual immorality, or of any kind of impurity, or of greed, because these are improper for God's holy people." Two unmarried people sleeping in the same tent together was more than a "hint" of sexual immorality, even if no actual sexual activity occurred.

Unless the Scriptures are the ultimate, overarching, final authority in our affairs in the church, our relationships with one another can quickly degenerate into little more than a shouting match or a blatant power play. On a broader scale, when the authority of God's Word is no longer the guiding rule of a church or society, the group is headed toward a rendezvous with chaos.

Don't Play Solitaire

Charles Lindbergh became a hero for his daring feat of crossing the Atlantic alone in a small plane. But by his own admission, it was a risky, nearly fatal venture. He had gotten little sleep the night before he took off. After hours of monotonous flying, his eyelids started to droop.

He awoke from his stupor to discover the wings on his plane were almost completely iced over. He began preparations for a crash landing in the ocean. Then he had an idea. In a last ditch maneuver, he pointed the nose of his plane down until he was just above the water. He knew the air was warmest there. Sure enough, the ice soon melted on his wings, and he was able to regain a safe altitude.

There's good reason why Lindbergh was named "Lucky Lindy." He came close to getting himself killed in a reckless solo venture.

Pastors and church leaders run the same danger when they deal with church problems on their own. Again, Leith Anderson has some words of advice:

> We [as a staff] don't handle things alone. We won't break a confidence, but no one, including me, handles significant matters by themselves. If we discover someone is dealing on their own with a possible suicide case or an incest situation, we crack down on them. Some problems

in ministry are just too difficult, and too dangerous, to negotiate alone.[4]

I was sound asleep one night when the phone rang next to my bed. Groggy and wanting six more hours of sleep, I reached over and groped for the receiver.

"Pastor, this is Flora. You better get over here right away. You know how my son-in-law killed himself yesterday? Now my daughter says she's going to kill herself."

This inner-city family had just experienced a tragedy. They woke up one morning to find their son-in-law hanging by an extension cord in the stairway. A victim of alcohol abuse, he had become depressed the night before and just decided to end his life. Now, his twenty-year-old grieving widow, who also abused alcohol, was intent on joining him in a reunion suicide. They lived in one of the toughest neighborhoods in the city, and I could tell by Flora's slurred speech she had been drinking, too.

"Flora, I'll be over as soon as I can. But I'm going to bring some people with me," I said. As soon as I hung up, I called a pastor who specializes in urban ministry. He graciously consented to meet me at the apartment building where they lived. Next, I called our deacon chairman and woke him up. He also agreed to accompany me.

Once we arrived, I was glad I hadn't gone it alone. When we got off the elevator, we were immediately met by Flora. "Where the _____ have you been?" she snarled at me. Their was a strong smell of whiskey on her breath. She was normally a polite and cheerful woman, so the personality change was a tip-off things were out of control.

I sat down next to the young grieving widow. Flora again entered the room and pointed toward her husband, who sat at the dining room table. "You know, pastor," she said. "He has a gun." Her two little boys on the couch nodded it was true. Daddy had a revolver.

I glanced at my two colleagues and gulped. I remember thinking, *Cheryl isn't going to like this if I get shot.* Fortunately, the older and more experienced pastor took over. In a matter of minutes, he had calmed everyone down. No gun was ever produced. We eventually were able to pray with the widow and get her to promise us she would not attempt suicide. Two nights later, I was involved in her husband's funeral at a local rescue mission.

Not every crisis in the church is that potentially dangerous, but it's pure foolishness to take on alone significant emergencies that have the potential for serious consequences. A good rule to follow is this: If I'm facing a situation that could impact a much larger group than just me, I need to get more people involved. Proverbs says it best: "Make plans by seeking advice; if you wage war, obtain guidance" (Prov. 20:18).

The *Smithsonian Magazine* carried an article on unexploded munitions in rural France. It's estimated that there are at least eight to twelve million unexploded shells and bombs, many containing poisonous gas, left in France from the two world wars. The government of France has hired an elite group of individuals to scour fields and forests and remove these left-over live munitions. They are called "de-miners."

While one has to admire their bravery, the truth is 638 of their group have been killed since 1946, the year they began their deadly clean-up. According to the article, last year alone five men were killed and a dozen wounded by everything from leaking mustard gas shells to buried shrapnel ordnance.

In a real sense, some issues in the church are potential munitions waiting to explode. Problems such as sexual indiscretion, child abuse, financial fraud, suicide, severe mental illness, and criminal behavior are the equivalent of live mustard gas shells. While it may seem heroic for a pastor or church leader to try and deal with these on his own, it's also foolish. Chances are, he will have his name on a memorial plaque before long.

We need other people in the church to help keep us from charging off on our own. Otherwise we may end up looking very foolish.

I was playing miniature golf with my wife shortly after we were married. I managed to bring a competitive spirit to what should have been a purely relaxing recreational event.

That night, the miniature golf course announced a special contest. "The next player who makes a hole-in-one with an orange ball will receive a special prize."

I looked down at the putting green. I had an orange golf ball. This was my moment. My one chance to win it all.

I took careful aim, tapped the ball with my putter, and watched with Arnold Palmer-like intensity as it rolled underneath the rotating windmill toward the hole. I couldn't see where it went.

"You did it!" Cheryl cried from the other side of the windmill. "A hole-in-one!"

Adrenaline surged through my body. I grabbed my ball and broke into a sprint toward the counter. I bounded over various holes. I hurdled across the greens, my putter waving over my head like a war club.

Somewhere between the ninth and tenth hole, I suddenly realized everyone had quit playing miniature golf and was staring at me. Just what was I doing? I sheepishly lowered the putter and casually walked the remaining distance to the counter.

"Uh, I'm the guy who got a hole-in-one," I mumbled to the attendant. I looked over at my wife. She was bent over with laughter. He handed me a ticket worth thirty-five cents off the next game.

The value of dealing with problems as a staff, rather than individually, is perspective. Other people can keep us from the equivalent of leaping across golf courses wildly waving a putter above our heads.

In All Fairness

Perhaps the final, if not most important, reason to adopt a systems approach is fairness and justice.

We recognize in our judicial system that it's possible for an individual judge or jury to abuse their power, to misapply the law, or to deny someone their Constitutional rights. That's why we have courts of appeal, all the way up to the Supreme Court.

In the same way, pastors or boards who lack recognized standards and guidelines for dealing with problems run the risk of abusing their power. They may be too heavy-handed in one case, and too lenient in another. Fairness is more likely to be accomplished when justice is handled by a group, rather than just one individual.

But even when a church has established standards, problems can occur that require an apology. Howard Clark tells of an incident where the church had to go back and make amends.

It was the "wedding season" and the pressure was on! The facilities were taxed and the staff overworked, but in the midst of this chaos was the steady constant, our prenuptial drill sergant, the wedding hostess.

She was always in command, never at a loss as to proper decorum, and had held the job since the Reformation. With three weddings on some Saturdays, we had to be efficient, and "Sarge" kept us running by the book. She had a reputation for being heavy-handed with people, but because she had held the job for years, no one challenged her.

On a particularly hot and muggy Saturday, a large wedding was about to begin—the marriage of a pastoral staff member. The residents of a local nursing home where he had ministered decided to make the wedding their outing for the month.

Just as the procession was about to begin, Sarge discovered one of the nursing home residents slumped over in her wheelchair. Assuming the person was seriously ill, she ordered her removed from the sanctuary at once.

The woman in the wheelchair had just fallen asleep. All the commotion attracted the attention of the senior associate pastor. When he found out what had happened he fired Sarge on the spot.

This was not the first time she had angered or reprimanded visitors. During a large musical performance she had scolded a woman saving a seat for her husband while he parked the car.

"Can't you read?" she said, "The ticket says no reserved seating." Of course the ticket merely served to remind everyone that our policy was open seating; it didn't preclude saving a seat for a relative or friend. But to Sarge, what was written was law! And her interpretation was the final word.

Sarge's firing was done in haste and without consultation, but the deacons stood by the decision. They knew it should have come long before this. While surgically quick and clean, her termination left gaping wounds in her life.

Word quickly spread that a dear and faithful servant had been wronged. The congregation saw us as culprits and her as a victim. While it may have been right, it was done in the wrong way.

We ended up having to retreat. Several deacons and myself went to her home and spent three hours listening to her recount her years of service to the church. It turned out this role was the one place in her life she had significance. She lived for wedding rehearsals and cere- monies and the opportunity to direct traffic in the sanc- tuary.

She justified her inflexible behavior by reminding us that in God's house, things should be done with decency and order. Underneath it all, however, was an obvious need for power, recognition, and significance, though it's doubtful she could have ever recognized that.

We asked her forgiveness. We had erred in stripping her of her position in such a abrupt manner. Hindsight is always so much more focused.

Instead of firing her immediately, we should have said, "I think the pressures of this job are more than you're able to handle. Let's find another way to use your skills." We did eventually find another position for her at the visi- tors' center. It helped restore her sense of position in the church.[5]

Sometimes it will be necessary to discuss your disciplinary actions with the congregation. That can be dangerous in itself, and you ought to get good legal advice before airing publicly action taken privately. But when it needs to be done to clear the air and insure fairness and justice, it should be done carefully and lovingly.

Conclusion

Several years ago the Super Bowl was held at the Silver Dome near Detroit, Michigan. It was the chance of a lifetime for many residents of the Motor City to attend the premier event in football. But many of those who purchased tickets never got to see the game. The event planners had set up a time-consuming and unnecessary process of getting people through the parking gates. On average, it took forty-five seconds to purchase a ticket and get into the lot. That resulted in massive back-ups on the roadways. Many frustrated and fuming fans had to settle for listening to the game on their car radio while holding a pair of crumpled Super Bowl tickets in hand.

Systems do matter, and they are ultimately made up of people who make either good or bad decisions. While conflict is a fact of life in every church, much unnecessary conflict can be avoided by establishing good systems. Establishing clear standards, clearly communicating expectations, using a group process to deal with difficult issues, and insisting on fairness and justice are key elements of building unity and unleashing harmony in the church.

Notes

1. Norm Shawchuck, "Case Study: The Entrenched and Ineffective Worker," *Leadership Journal* 14 (Summer 1993):66.

2. Personal interview with Leith Anderson.

3. Ibid.

4. Ibid.

5. Howard Clark, "Case Study: The Entrenched and Ineffective Worker," *Leadership Journal* 14 (Summer 1993):73-74.

What Prayer and Fasting Can Accomplish

Besides adopting a systems approach to prevent or deal with conflicts, churches must utilize spiritual resources to deal with spiritual problems, not just in crisis, but as a regular part of their life together. In some situations, only the direct intervention of God can restore unity and harmony to a church. How can we draw on the power of the Holy Spirit to mend the fractures of a broken congregation? Pastor David Henson tells his own remarkable story of the healing of Church of the Foothills.

"God has blessed this church in ways that are impossible to describe," says Pastor Henson. "We are beginning to experience genuine revival as a process. The wind of the Spirit of God is blowing in a marvelous fashion."

It wasn't always that way for Church of the Foothills, a Baptist congregation in eastern Texas. When Henson first arrived at the church, he found a congregation demoralized, divided, and filled with despair.

A Spiritual Air Inversion

There was something unusual about the atmosphere at Church of the Foothills. It was if a spiritual smog hung over the church, polluting the atmosphere with despair and discouragement. "There was at times a foul odor in the building that was unexplainable," remembers Henson. "It would come and go without cause. It was a wretched smell, a septic tank odor. I began praying, and asked a select group of other individuals to pray, that this smell would dissipate."

It wasn't just inside the building people sensed something was wrong. "I had people tell me that even when they drove into our long driveway they begin to experience a spirit of despair, darkness, an emotional depression. It wasn't just one individual. Several people independent of each other told me the same thing."

Henson experienced the same phenomenon himself. "I remember driving up the expressway one morning and looking over at our property. I could literally see darkness hovering above our building. My inner response was, 'I don't want to go into that place. I want out of here.' That was precisely what the Adversary wanted me to feel."

But Henson wisely chose to keep these matters of spiritual discernment and inner struggles to himself. He never mentioned them publicly to the congregation. Instead, Henson attempted to maintain as positive and faith-filled a posture as possible. The pulpit was not the place to tell the people of his suspicions that the church was in the grip of a stronghold of darkness.

"It's important for a pastor not to be dismayed before the people," he says. "We must be careful not to share our suspicions and intuitions in unwise ways. I was able to maintain leadership by not sharing these struggles with the congregation."

Abundant Strife

But to even casual observers, there were signs something was seriously wrong at Church of the Foothills. The church had been through a series of short pastorates. The staff members were frequently besieged by criticism from certain members. The church was known in the community as a place of internal acrimony and fierce clashes. Sunday was such a day of contention that some previous pastors requested prayer just for them to make it through the day.

The life and energy of Church of the Foothills was also sapped by a shadow government of unelected individuals who operated independently of elected boards and officials. Board meetings, congregational meetings, even private encounters were often scenes of ugly infighting.

Pastor Henson received numerous letters from individuals who attacked his character and ministry. Some were so biting and belligerent he could scarcely believe one Christian could say such things to another believer.

Previous pastors had suffered in a similar fashion from these guerrilla tactics. In the face of what appeared to be both a visible and invisible struggle, Pastor Henson began to pray and fast. He asked others to do the same. Together, they began to ask God to lift the invisible blanket of despair.

"I would even pray out loud as I entered the building and my office, though of course no one could hear me. I also discreetly requested others to pray for the cleansing of our building and the release of our congregation from this dark hand of oppression."

Nowhere was that sense of oppression more palpable to the discerning than in the sanctuary on Sunday morning.

"There was this sense of corporate sadness in the worship service that I couldn't explain," says Henson. "I began to wonder if the sanctuary itself might contain an element of unseen darkness. My level of concern was raised when my brother-in-law, who came to visit us one Sunday, called me after he returned home.

"David, I could see in your face and sense in the worship service a heaviness," he said.

"What do you mean?" I asked.

"I sensed something awful and unseen in the sanctuary," he said.

"Where?"

"In the ceiling area above the platform," he replied. "Directly above the piano, organ, and pulpit."

"Richard, that's exactly where I've experienced it," Henson replied.

Henson had to work hard to keep his balance during this difficult time. "I had to be careful not to give the impression I was on some type of hunt for the demonic. A fixation on evil spirits is not a hallmark of a healthy ministry, nor is it part of my theological tradition. But I did express quietly to trusted friends the need to pray about these specific situations."

During this time, Henson again received numerous ugly and threatening phone calls. "On my voice mail I received several anonymous calls that included a direct death threat. I had to take that seriously, so I went to the police department. The police listened to the recordings. I remember the police sergeant saying, 'I don't know who you're dealing with, but it's an intensely angry, volatile individual.' "

The messages were often vile. Some included explicit sexual remarks, and others intimidating threats against Pastor Henson. He was never able to recognize the voices involved. To further harass him, Henson received hundreds of anonymous hang-ups.

But was this all just his imagination? Or was he facing a serious spiritual offensive aimed at driving him out and rendering Church of the Foothills spiritually inoperative?

"This much I'm certain of—Satan's chief goal is to rob God of glory," he says. "One way he accomplishes that is the invisible work of his forces in the midst of a society that doesn't believe they exist. But as we know from Scripture, all true battles are fought in the spiritual world."

Henson received some reassuring counsel from respected outsiders that the spiritual war raging in his church was indeed a reality. "On one occasion a well-known church consultant was working in our area. He had heard of the problems in our congregation and decided to just drive by our property. Later, he told me, 'When I turned onto the property, I was so overwhelmed by the sense of the demonic, that I stopped my car. I sat there for almost ten minutes. When I finally left, I said to myself, "This place is a spiritual shell." ' "

The Tide Begins to Turn

Shortly after their conversation, two significant events took place at Church of the Foothills that began to change the course of the unseen battle.

The first was the result of a special series of sermons Henson preached. "I spent several weeks preaching on prayer and fasting. At the close of the series, I mentioned that we as a church were in need of both forgiveness and deliverance from the unnecessary spiritual baggage we seemed saddled with.

"I suggested we pray and fast and ask God to grant us a spirit of repentance, confession, oneness, restoration, responsibility, and accountability in a gracious and loving way. Not everyone took up the challenge, but a number of people did. I asked those individuals eager to commit themselves to a ministry of prayer and fasting to please stand." A significant number rose to their feet.

Not long after that, the spiritual smog started to lift at Church of the Foothills. "God's Spirit began to manifest himself in some delightful ways," remembers Henson. "He began working in worship, in relationships, and in individual witness. People began finding freedom over long-term habits they could not conquer. The strongholds of hopelessness began to fall."

The second juncture in the road to spiritual freedom and reconciliation came almost a year later. "There was a window of time when a number of people, for reasons good or bad, no longer felt comfortable to continue to worship with us. They left and went elsewhere. During that same period, God seemed to open the door to outsiders and numerous visitors appeared."

Had Henson prayed that certain people would leave? "Absolutely not. I never prayed, nor did anyone else, that certain people would go elsewhere. We only asked God to make us a deeper, not larger congregation. We prayed for a concentrated interest in exalting Christ, not ourselves. How God chose to answer that prayer involved a number of people leaving."

But the most profound change during this time was not a change in the make-up of the congregation, but a transformation in the soul of Pastor Henson.

"My own spiritual learning curve shot straight up. Because of all the difficulties I had been through at Church of the Foothills, I found it hard to love the church as I wished to. I had felt unloved at times, so unfortunately, I had allowed that to dampen my affection for the people."

But Henson's lukewarm heart was about to be re-ignited—on the expressway of all places. "One day, as I was driving home from church, I broke down and began to weep. I wept so hard I couldn't see the road. I cried out to the Lord to forgive me for my lack of love for my church. I asked him to give me the new heart of a shepherd. I wanted to love my sheep.

"In near instantaneous fashion, my heart seemed filled with an overwhelming sense of peace. I looked at the other drivers on the road and found myself feeling love toward them. As one car after another passed, I started to say, 'I love you.'" His heart was filled with a hilarious sense of joy and compassion. He looked at one motorist and said, "You don't know it, buddy, but I love you, too."

New Pastor, Same Person

Henson perceived a connection between his spiritual revival and the renewal now taking place in his congregation.

"I experienced a new level of compassion and strength to shepherd my people. I was able to be both strong and tender toward my people at the same time. Up till then, I had felt misunderstood and even rejected at times as a pastor. God began to grant me favor in the eyes of the people."

The revival that had taken place in Henson's heart spread through the congregation. It even reached into the former stronghold of despair, the sanctuary and the worship service.

"Our worship on Sunday became filled with joy, praise, and anticipation," says Henson. "For some time Church of the Foothills had the reputation of formality and stiffness. It began to be known as a place of joy, refreshment, and genuine spontaneity in the Spirit. Today, there's a tremendous sense of the presence of the Lord Jesus Christ."

Because of the dramatic changes that prayer and fasting had led to, the church decided to make both an intensive part of their worship strategy. "We began each Sunday to gather a group early in the morning to pray for the worship service. We prayed for all aspects of the day, even for the presence of the Holy Spirit to begin working in people's lives as they pulled into our driveway."

Did God answer their parking lot petitions? "We soon noticed that people entered our building smiling. When I would look out from the pulpit, I would no longer see sad and forlorn expressions. Instead, I began to see a brightness in people's eyes. Our singing became powerful. It's a rich experience to stand next to someone who is singing with all their heart."

Whereas Henson used to receive harsh and discouraging notes, the nature of his correspondence began to reflect the renewal of Church of the Foothills.

"I started to receive scores of notes on a weekly basis from people who explained how God was working in their lives through his Word. If there was a complaint, it was that our worship service went by much too quickly."

Battle Scars

But there had been a cost to such a long and protracted battle. Henson had almost lost his health and his ministry during the darkest months of the ordeal.

"I had moved from despair to despondency into actual depression," remembers Henson. "But in a moment of spiritual healing, the depression was removed from my life."

One conviction helped keep Henson going through the experience. "I always had a strong sense that God had called me here. As G. K. Chesterton once said, 'The difference between a radical and a reformer is that a reformer knows what he is doing while he is undoing.' "

Henson doesn't think his church's struggle is a unique case. "I believe spiritual warfare is the underlying explanation for the darkness and strife that engulfs so many congregations."

Carl George, a well-known and respected church conflict consultant, agrees with Henson's conclusion. He believes that disruption from the unseen spiritual world is by far the most common source of conflict in the church.

"Jesus taught his disciples to pray, 'Thy kingdom come, thy will be done, on earth as it is in heaven,' " he says. "We have a very naive view of what that means. A vision of the kingdom of God that is free of struggle is an apocalyptic vision (of the future) which is not yet attained in our experience in life."

He points to the story of the angelic messenger sent to reach Daniel during the time of the exile. After three weeks of mourning, fasting, and prayer, the angel was at last able to break through to him. Upon his arrival he said,

Do not be afraid, Daniel. Since the first day that you set

your mind to gain understanding and to humble yourself before your God, your words were heard, and I have come in response to them. But the prince of the Persian kingdom resisted me twenty-one days. Then Michael, one of the chief princes, came to help me, because I was detained there with the king of Persia. Now I have come to explain to you what will happen to your people in the future, for the vision concerns a time yet to come (Dan. 10:12-14).

Paul makes a similar allusion in the New Testament to spiritual warfare occurring in the heavenly places,

For our struggle is not against flesh and blood, but against the rulers, against the authorities, against the powers of this dark world and against the spiritual forces of evil in the heavenly realms. Therefore put on the full armor of God, so that when the day of evil comes, you may be able to stand your ground, and after you have done everything, to stand (Eph. 6:12-13).

Henson's church, through prayer and fasting, found the strength to stand together. A moment of great celebration occurred when Church of the Foothills was asked to host a regional conference on spiritual victory in Christ.

"Representatives from over two hundred churches attended the meetings in our church," says Henson. "We concluded the conference with a Friday night worship celebration and communion service in our sanctuary. That night there was an overwhelming sense of the brightness of the Spirit of God. It turned out to be the most powerful worship experience I had ever been involved in. As I looked around our worship center, I was reminded of the cleansing power of the blood of Jesus. I thought, 'How unbelievable. Just a few years ago, this building groaned under the weight of oppression. Now it's a place of joy, celebration, power, and the magnificence of God.' "

The changes that prayer and fasting brought to Church of
the Foothills were explained in a note Henson received from one
of his parishioners.

There are so many positive and exciting things being
said within the congregation. We are learning a multitude of lessons. Fasting and prayer has long been something I've personally practiced. When I do fast, I have to
spend another day just to thank God for all the answers
and blessings I receive. It's incredible how close this practice brings me to the Lord. I hear him speaking to me in
love, warmth, and personal direction.

Looking back, Henson is convinced that fasting and prayer
permitted the daylight to once again break through on Church of
the Foothills. "That proved to be the end of darkness and the
opening of the door to the Spirit of God."

What Is a Fast?

Fasting is the practice of going without food or water (or
both) for a time to devote one's self to prayer and communion
with God. It is temporarily giving up something of physical value
to have something of spiritual value put in its place.

Jesus assumed his followers would fast. In the Sermon on the
Mount he says, "But *when you fast*, put oil on your head and wash
your face, so that it will not be obvious to men that you are fasting, but only to your Father, who is unseen; and your Father, who
sees what is done in secret, will reward you" (Matt. 6:17-18).

There are a variety of fasts, including a partial fast and a total
fast. A partial fast involves giving up food for a limited time,
while continuing to take liquids. This may mean missing breakfast and lunch, then perhaps breaking the fast with something
light in the midafternoon or for supper.

A total fast is when an individual takes in neither food nor water. Since the human body requires water to function, this should be done only for a short interval of time (perhaps a day or two), and only with the advice of a physician.

As Henson points out, major figures in both the Old and New Testament practiced fasting. The results were always powerful and transformational. "There is not one single episode of an individual praying and fasting in the New Testament where God did not respond," Henson says. Jesus, Paul, Peter, John, the apostles, and a variety of others fasted.

Carl George believes prayer with fasting is a discipline churches need in order to deal with serious conflict, "Flat out, it's the largest, single solution to the majority of divisive problems I've seen in the church. But a breakthrough occurs only when somebody decides to pay the price in prayer."

George is concerned that many churches don't see the importance of prayer and fasting in protecting or releasing their churches from conflict. The problem is many believers have a worldview that doesn't leave room for spiritual warfare.

Unfortunately, many church leaders and members in America hold a worldview that contains what missiologists now call the "vacant middle." They are essentially deists in their world view. For them, the space between a distant transcendental God in heaven and human activity on earth—the space in between is not populated by angels or devils, but is vacant. Because they don't wish to see the demonic working near at hand, they religate them to some far, remote place. The fact is, there are spirits, spiritual forces, and spiritual personalities very near and very much at work. It takes prayer to break the power of evil.

Henson's experience of facing corporate "depression" in worship doesn't surprise George. "I have been in sanctuaries that groaned and creaked under the weight of the dark angels," he says. Though evil may be a reality, George is confident of the authority believers possess in Jesus Christ to gain victory according to God's Word.

"The weapons of our warfare are not carnal, but mighty through God to the pulling down of strong holds," he says. He recommends believers learn to cleanse territories, to walk the sanctuary, to pace the grounds, and to spend long hours in prayer over a church facility and congregation asking God for his protection and direction. "You must organize prayer people and instruct them to pray for the pastor and the church during significant events. You need the protection such prayer provides."

To ignore the realities of spiritual warfare can leave a local church in a perilous situation. "You can end up in a powerless church where the evil has become entrenched. It will not leave except by prayer and fasting over some period of time," says George.

How can a pastor organize such effective prayer groups to do battle on behalf of the church? George believes in the necessity of developing "base communities" in the local church. "These are cells, small groups, or classes no larger than a dozen people. It provides for mutual self-care and a place where the truth can be spoken in love."

He sees these base communities or small groups as a place where true spiritual health can be fostered. "We need solitude, where we have time to hear God. We need community, where we have the opportunity to bear one another's burdens. And we need simplicity, where we get materialism out of our lives and focus on real values."

George sees an analogy between early eighteenth-century

England and modern society. "We're at the same place John Wesley was when he started class meetings. The disruptions of the normal family ties as industrialization created by large scale employment dislocation made it a terrible time. Yet, his class meetings gave people a way of finding themselves, finding God, finding community, and finding faith. His movement became a stabilizing factor for the entire nation."

A Call to Arms and Folded Hands

Both Henson and George agree that churches must rise to the challenge of the day. "Like it or not," George says, "we are in a battle. And like it or not, the unseen forces do not respond to anything except the Word of God. The way back from conflict for a church lies in group and corporate prayer as much as any other single factor. It is in those types of prayer groups that people see each other's hearts. It is there they come to understand that the awesome power of God is available to us in the here and now. It is there we see our faith is worthwhile."

Whereas prayer and fasting can provide the power for a significant spiritual breakthrough, sometimes the answer to renewal and reconciliation starts with a simple apology. As we'll see in the next chapter, when a church does confess its sin and wrongdoing, just about anything can happen next.

CHAPTER 10

The Value of Saying "I'm Sorry"

Ridgeview Church, a congregation in the Pacific Northwest, went almost two years before it could locate someone willing to risk taking the job of senior pastor. Ridgeview had gained the unwelcome reputation of roughing up pastors. More than one minister had left feeling like he had endured a nonstop prize fight without the benefit of gloves or a referee.

The leadership of Ridgeview wanted to end this negative relationship with its pastors, but wasn't certain where to begin. Jim Isaacs, a newer member of the board, believed it was scripturally wrong for these relationships to end on such a sour note. It also didn't make sense. Ridgeview was located in a community heavily populated by well-educated engineers and computer analysts. Such professionals were certainly capable of building positive relationships in the church, just as they did in the business world.

A History of Perpetual Commotion

Isaacs and other church leaders began to research the history of Ridgeview, and discovered a disturbing pattern. "We've had a history of strong pastors and strong opposition in the congregation. When a disagreement between the board and the pastor got started, both positions would seem to harden."

Their research also led them to a fascinating revelation. "We discovered certain issues seemed to reoccur every few years. Once the problem got going, it always seemed to follow the same course. It always ended in the pastor leaving hurt and wounded. So I began to campaign our elder board to address this issue."

As a first step in the reconciliation process, Isaacs and others persuaded the board to contact previous pastors. "We wrote to former pastors and asked them what the church had done to wound them," he says. "Each pastor had left under different circumstances, so we tried to find different individuals in the church who knew the history of each situation. We then wrote a letter of reconciliation to former pastors asking forgiveness for the pain we had caused them as a church."

The board received back letters of appreciation and forgiveness from these former pastors. The pastors indicated how much the board's gesture had meant to them. It was a significant step toward healing.

A Divine Appointment at Thirty Thousand Feet

It was shortly after this that Isaacs was on an airplane and met a man who had a profound influence on him. "I sat next to a biblical scholar who had written a small pamphlet on Solemn Assemblies. Both of us discovered we had an interest in the subject of revival. That discussion kindled my fire. When I got home, I began using his material in the church."

Just before the pastor at the time resigned, Isaacs suggested that the church consider holding their own Solemn Assembly. "We decided to use the pamphlet as the basis for designing a special worship service for the purpose of confession of sin. As a board, we developed a catalog of corporate sins we believed we had committed as a church."

Finally, the board agreed in principle to hold a Solemn Assembly. But they recognized a certain amount of groundwork was necessary to make the event effective. "We started five months before the service by focusing on prayer. We went to different Sunday school classes explaining to people what we were doing. We distributed the pamphlet on a Solemn Assembly and invited people to read it. At first all we received was a number of blank looks. But little by little, the church began to catch the concept."

Part of the process involved a self-examination of the way Ridgeview Church had conducted its affairs in the past. "We went through a process of understanding that corporate sin is just as much an offense to God as personal sin," says Isaacs. "We discovered that the way we conducted our business, the way we had used politics in the church, and the way we had talked about each other in the past was corporately sinful."

What are corporate sins? They are sins that the group, not just the individual, bear responsibility for. By virtue of membership in that group, everyone carries a certain accountability for allowing them to occur.

In the case of Ridgeview, some members had publicly called certain leaders in the church 'incompetent.' There had been gossip exchanged about the staff. Business meetings had often involved harsh debate.

"We needed to confess and repent of all these things," says Isaacs. "We wanted to bring them to closure. We knew it was important not to leave things unresolved."

A Session of Confession

The Solemn Assembly is an idea that dates back to the Old Testament. On several occasions the people of Israel were called together to confess their sins and the sins of their fathers. For example, we read of a Solemn Assembly that took place after the people of Israel returned from exile in Babylon:

On the twenty-forth day of the same month, the
Israelites gathered together, fasting and wearing sackcloth
and having dust on their heads [ancient symbols of
repentance]. Those of Israelite descent had separated
themselves from all foreigners. They stood in their places
and confessed their sins and the wickedness of their
fathers. They stood where they were and read from the
Book of the Law of the Lord their God for a quarter of
the day, and spent another quarter in confession and in
worshiping the Lord their God (Neh. 9:1-3).

When the Sunday evening of the Solemn Assembly at
Ridgeview arrived, between three hundred and four hundred
people turned out. "The spiritual core of the church seemed in
tune with it," says Isaacs. "We discovered there had been some
quiet saints who had been praying for this to happen. The board
led the service that night. We had spent hours and hours working
out the wording of what each person would say."

After a short time of introduction, the elders rose one by one
to read detailed confessions of corporate sin. Several themes were
developed that evening around various aspects of communal sin.
The list included such sins as an unloving spirit, critical and hurtful remarks, a lack of proper submission to biblical leadership, a
spirit of pride, rebellion, and gossip.

Because the emphasis was on corporate sin, the congregation
was asked to confess not only their wrongdoing, but the sins of
the fathers as well. Much like a modern concert of prayer, individuals were invited to pray aloud in response to each of these
themes. The people collectively asked for the forgiveness of God
and the restoration of relationships. Relevant portions of
Scripture were then read to assure the people of God's pardon
and willingness to forgive.

Isaacs and the others also began crafting a letter of apology to their current pastor. Once he agreed to its wording, it was read by one of the board members to the church during a later worship service.

How Successful Was It?

"I would describe a Solemn Assembly more as a process than an event," says Isaacs. "It didn't eradicate all the church's problems. But it did begin to change the tone of business meetings and the attitude people had toward the leadership.

"While we did not have what I consider a historic revival, we still corporately did what we needed to do. There are still pockets of resentment left—people who insist on having their own way—but we no longer have the outbursts we once had in congregational meetings."

There are those who see even more significant changes as a result of the Solemn Assembly. One of these is John Edwards, now the senior pastor at Ridgeview Church. Before coming to Ridgeview, he had heard of their legacy of conflict.

"I came to Ridgeview with my eyes wide open," says Edwards. "I knew it had a history of church splits, controversy over the discipline of members, and similar matters. I was frightened. So I asked the Lord for reassurance from his Word. I knew that unless the Lord blessed my time here, I could be chewed up and spit out quite easily."

Yet, from the day he arrived, Pastor Edwards began to see the impact of the Solemn Assembly on the life of the church. "In my first ten months we were able to change bylaws, establish a vision statement to promote unity and direction, and make other strategic changes. I sat back and marveled at how much had been done in such a short time. God directed me to Psalm 124 where the psalmist says, "Let Israel say, 'If the Lord had not been on our side...the flood would have engulfed us, the torrent would have swept over us, the raging waters would have swept us away.'"

Coupons of Reconciliation

Building on the success of the Solemn Assembly, Pastor Edwards suggested another novel idea to deal with the problems that still remained. He proposed a Forgiveness and Reconciliation seminar. "For several weeks we offered free coupons in the bulletin. The coupons essentially said, 'I believe there is a problem or something that separates us. Let's attend the Forgiveness and Reconciliation seminar, then meet with a third party to work this out.' We encouraged people to cut out the coupons, sign them, then give them to the other person involved."

Edwards carefully planned the event. He had arranged for two trained professionals to make presentations on forgiveness and reconciliation. They each spent considerable time explaining the biblical basis for forgiving another person, and how to find true restoration of relationships. They outlined practical steps for people to implement.

Those who had signed and returned the coupons were assigned to meet with a mediator in the afternoon. "We called these counselors, 'loyal yokefellows,' " says Edwards. "We based that concept on Philippians 4:2-3, 'I plead with Euodia and I plead with Syntyche to agree with each other in the Lord. Yes, and I ask you, loyal yokefellow, help these women who have contended at my side in the cause of the gospel, along with Clement and the rest of my fellow workers, whose names are in the book of life.' "

One hundred people showed up at the seminar, and several afternoon appointments were scheduled with "yokefellows." The results were encouraging. Some met together with the mediator, some alone. "The day proved to be another major breakthrough for the church," remembers Edwards.

Tension Relievers

As a next step toward creating a wholesome atmosphere for discussion and debate, Edwards and the board began holding information meetings. These were nonvoting meetings where people could meet to discuss issues and ask questions. "Our goal was to defuse tension and conflict before we actually got to a meeting where a vote would be taken."

Edwards also started using the bulletin to keep people better informed. He even took the unusual step of meeting with entire classes or small groups in homes to allow people to voice concerns and raise questions. When he became aware that two individuals were involved in significant conflict, he would call them to his office and meet with them in person.

Edwards recognized that Ridgeview had suffered from a corporate culture of unhealthy confrontation and methods of dealing with conflict. "Bitterness is a staining sin," he says. "It corrupts those around the bitter individual as Hebrews 12:15 points out. It becomes contagious and soon works its way through the entire Body. Satan gets a toehold, then a foothold, then a stronghold, then finally a stranglehold. When I came to Ridgeview, I could see the stranglehold bitterness had on some people."

A Cold Sunday of Warm Hearts

The many efforts of the leadership of the church to restore unity and make amends for past offenses led to an event that caught Edwards entirely by surprise. It had happened one cold and wintry Sunday morning.

"It was awesome," Edwards remembers. "I was preaching on Ecclesiastes 2, then at the end of the sermon I said, 'We need to do business with the Lord. I am inviting you to join with me in repenting of worldliness and committing ourselves to holiness and Christlikeness. If you're willing to do just that, please come forward and kneel at the front of the church.' "

The entire congregation came forward as one person. Once the front of the church was jam-packed, people knelt in the aisles. There were tears. There was brokenness. "It was a movement of the Holy Spirit of God," says Edwards. "When I gave the same invitation in the second service, the same thing happened. Everyone who could, came forward."

Afterward, a visitor came up to Edwards and said, "John, this just doesn't happen in Ridgeview." Still overwhelmed by the presence of the Holy Spirit, Pastor Edwards got up the next Sunday and asked the congregation, "What happened last Sunday? Help me understand it."

Several people filled out cards that explained what had happened in their lives. "I received over 150 responses from the people," says Edwards. "They mainly described the repentance that had occurred in their lives."

One card said, "I repented of the ill will I've had toward my brother." Another said, "I repented of my pride. I focused on making an image for myself and not caring for others." Some dealt with specific behaviors, such as, "I repented of my addiction to _____."

"It was a decisive time of healing in the church," says Edwards. In his private devotional time, Edwards asked God to help him understand what he was doing in his congregation.

"God led me to Isaiah 30: 'The moon will shine like the sun, and the sunlight will be seven times brighter, like the light of seven full days, when the Lord binds up the bruises of his people and heals the wounds he inflicted' (v. 26).

"I began to understand that a significant milestone had been achieved because people had committed themselves to the healing of the congregation with an act of their will." Edwards believed he received even a more remarkable promise that day. "The Lord also led me to Jeremiah 33:6-9, 'Nevertheless, I will bring health and healing to it; I will heal my people and will let them enjoy abundant peace and security. I will bring Judah and Israel back from captivity and will rebuild them as they were before. I will cleanse them from all the sin they have committed against me and will forgive all their sins of rebellion against me.'"

Edwards had for some time asked God to give him a great vision for Ridgeview. "That's when I read verse 9, 'Then this city will bring me renown, joy, praise and honor before all nations on earth that hear of all the good things I do for it; and they will be in awe and will tremble at the abundant prosperity and peace I provide for it.' "

Was it possible that Ridgeview could become a byword for repentance, healing, and restoration to replace its previous image as a place of division, acrimony, and short pastorates? Edwards believes it's a distinct possibility. "I felt the Lord was saying that he not only wants to bring healing to Ridgeview Church, but to all churches in this community."

What about the Future?

The final chapter has not been written on Ridgeview Church. Jim Isaacs worries that the church might all too easily slip back to its previous pattern of strong leadership and strong resistance. Pastor Edwards acknowledges there are still hurdles to clear in restoring unity and health to the congregation.

But both believe something began the day the church chose to apologize and began making amends for past sins. The results of such humility and contrition are outlined in 2 Chronicles 7:14, " 'If my people, who are called by name, will humble themselves and pray and seek my face and turn from their wicked ways, then will I hear from heaven and will forgive their sin and will heal their land.' "

A Pastor Is a Terrible Thing to Waste

It is said that up to a week after the famous battle of Waterloo in 1812, there were still wounded men left lying on the battlefield. There were no hospitals, no surgeons, not so much as an orderly to offer these gallant, fallen soldiers a final drink of water.

The local church can sometimes resemble such a battlefield. When the smoke clears and the two sides retreat, wounded and hurting people are left behind with no one to care for them. More often than not, the pastor and his wife are among the neglected casualties.

Steve Fullcroft was one such victim. When conflict in his Florida church escalated to the point he was forced from the pulpit, he eventually resigned and left the ministry. Years of rigorous education, valuable pastoral experience, and a shepherd's caring heart were all about to be lost.

That's when a small church with a heart for wounded pastors contacted Steve and his wife. Their innovative Pastor in Residence program picked Steve up off the battlefield and carried him to a place of safety. In this chapter, Steve tells his story—the remarkable recounting of one church that believed a pastor is a terrible thing to waste.

The Gathering Clouds

I was putting away my sermon notes one night after the evening service when I noticed the light on under the door of an elder's office. That wasn't unusual. As a volunteer staff member, this elder often put in long hours at the church. I decided to just put my head in the door to say goodnight, but when I opened it I was left speechless. There sat assembled in front of me the entire official board, meeting in an unscheduled and secret session.

Stunned by the sight, I groped for words. The board members were equally unnerved by my chance discovery of the meeting. Their faces conveyed both embarrassment and guilt—and with good reason. They had been caught with their hands in the cookie jar of church politics. After we exchanging a few awkward pleasantries, I excused myself and hurried out of the church.

I shouldn't have been all that surprised by the incident. It fit into a larger pattern of growing mistrust and deteriorating communication between the board and myself which had been accelerating for several months. Just a few weeks earlier one elder had called me a "habitual liar" in front of the entire group. He went on to accuse my children of the same character pathology—a trait he informed me, he suspected they had learned from their father.

By the time things reached bottom, I found myself forced from my pulpit, denied the opportunity to say goodbye to my congregation, and left to recover from a series of unjustified character attacks.

In all the confusion and hurt that followed my resignation, I was certain of this much—I never wanted to pastor another church as long as I lived.

Demoralized by the experience, angered by the abuse I had received, and squeezed by the financial pressures of providing for my family, I began seeking work in the business world. I was offered a job by both an insurance company and the IRS, which suited me just fine. As far as I was concerned I was through with the ministry.

But God had a much different resolution to the pain and anguish I had suffered.

Through the unexpected intervention of an innovative pastor I had never met before, a compassionate congregation willing to take a chance on a stranger, and an unorthodox program called the Pastor in Residence, a wounded and broken minister was restored to the ministry.

Beware of Sheep Asked to Leave the Fold

I had accepted the call to Brentwood Community Church in Florida filled with zeal and optimism. Brentwood was recovering from the devastating impact of a pastor's moral lapse. They had shrunk in size from a church of eight hundred people to a little under two hundred members by the time I arrived.

I wasted no time in throwing myself into the work. My wife and I soon fell in love with the people. Emotionally I was on a high. Filled with joy and optimism, the church began a dramatic turn-around. Within four years the church attendance stood at about three hundred people, conversions were a weekly occurrence, and the wounds from the past appeared to be rapidly healing.

But my enthusiasm couldn't compensate for my naiveté. I failed to see the gathering clouds of spiritual warfare on the horizon. I didn't understand the value of asking people questions about their lives that go beyond their theological convictions. And, perhaps most unrealistically of all, I assumed if problems arose with the leadership, they would always be worked out in an amiable and godly fashion.

Things were continuing to go extraordinarily well when several families began visiting from another church. They were open about the fact they had been asked to leave their previous congregation by the board. I never took the time to ask why they had been shown the door, but looking back now, I wish I had.

At first the new families were very supportive and enthusiastic toward me. They seemed overjoyed to have found the home they were looking for—a congregation that would love and accept them just as they were. They threw themselves into the life of the church. Given their high level of commitment, two men were eventually elected to the official board.

Yet, there was a problem with each family that caused me some concern. They seemed to have trouble accepting the shortcomings and imperfections in other people. This was particularly true in matters of secondary doctrine or lifestyle. They displayed little patience, tolerance, or forbearance with those who didn't meet their standards of behavior or belief.

As they gained influence in the church, the atmosphere became increasingly stifling and intolerant.

My wife was the first to see the implications of the creeping rigidity that was taking over the congregation. Somewhat prophetically she said one evening, "Steve, we're not going to last very long in this present climate."

I shrugged off her comment, believing I could work out any problem that might arise with people. After all, we were all reasonable men committed to doing God's work in God's way.

The first real confrontation occurred over a divorce issue. A couple from our church had separated, and despite our efforts to bring reconciliation, they dissolved their marriage. The wife left the church, while the husband stayed on, hurting and in need of fellowship. For solace and companionship, he turned to our single's group.

Immediately, one new board member objected.

"Our single's ministry is for people who have never married or are widowed, not for people going through a divorce," he argued. "Furthermore, I don't think he should be allowed to sing in the choir. We have to maintain our standards if we expect our church to be blessed."

"Frank," I replied, "this person neither committed adultery nor deserted his spouse. I don't believe in divorce any more than you do. But he's a member of the body and we need to reach out to him at this critical point in his life."

The person was unyielding. The man had to leave the single's group and the choir—now. He received support for his hard line from another new board member.

"I'm concerned about the purity of our church, aren't you pastor?" the second man asked.

From that day onward, a hairline fracture began to emerge between those two men and me. It would eventually open up into a breach of distrust and acrimony the size of the San Andreas Fault.

Under pressure from these two, I was instructed to relay the bad news to the divorced man that he could no longer attend the single's group or sing in the choir.

I felt caught in the middle. On the one hand, I was spending significant time with the divorced man trying to encourage him. He needed my help and compassion after such a traumatic experience. On the other hand, I was accountable to the board to carry out their directives. That meant telling him he was no longer welcome in certain ministries in the church.

I balked at the thought of hitting him with such hard news with little warning. When I did meet with him, I softened the news by telling him there were concerns about his involvement at church due to his divorce. But I stopped short of saying he was forbidden from ever taking part in those two groups again.

When I reported on my conversation, the two board

members were upset. They insisted I meet with him again and tell him exactly what had been decided. This time I took great pains to follow their directions. I conveyed the hard news to my friend just as it was. As far as I was concerned, I had done their bidding and the issue was resolved.

All appeared to be well until about three months later. During an elder meeting, one of the two men looked straight at me and said, "Steve, I'm concerned that you have a character problem in your life."

"What is it?" I asked, startled by his comment.

"I think you're a habitual liar," he said in a matter-of-fact voice. "Not only that, but so is your five-year-old boy. I think he may be picking it up from you."

Emotionally, I felt as if I had just stepped on a land mine. I was blown away. Though I didn't react outwardly, it took several minutes for me to recover my composure.

I had never considered myself perfect, but this was the first time in my life some had ever questioned my integrity. I knew I had blind spots in my life, but never for a moment did I consider myself a chronic liar.

For days my head seemed to spin. Was it true? Was I a habitual liar? Why hadn't anyone, including my wife, ever raised such a concern? What in the world was going on here?

A Prisoner in My Own Parish

It was only a few weeks after this traumatic confrontation that I stumbled onto the board in secret session. When we met for a scheduled meeting a week later, I confronted the group with my deep hurt and disappointment over their actions.

"Gentlemen," I began that evening, "I've always believed that we could work out problems openly and honestly. What you did meeting without me lacked basic integrity."

Too ashamed to argue, they apologized. But the reconciliation proved short-lived. Communication between us became more and more strained. Soon I found myself watching my every word, whether in private conversation or from the pulpit. To guard against further attacks on my credibility, I felt compelled to document everything—from memos to announcements to telephone calls.

Rightly or wrongly, I had the distinct sense I was being watched. I became a prisoner in my own church. My joy and freedom in ministry had been taken captive.

Sadly, the congregation knew little or nothing of what was occurring between the board and me. But as tensions mounted, my passion for preaching diminished. I was too emotionally distracted to give my best to the congregation. Instead, I was haunted by questions such as, "Am I really a liar? Do I actually lack the integrity to be a pastor? Have I been so self-deceived for so long?"

I found it demeaning to sit in my office hour after hour, like a lonely soldier dug-in deep in hostile territory, keeping logs and checking records. My attention was focused entirely on survival, trying to protect myself from the next possible attack on my character.

The siege-mentality was taking its toll on me. Slowly but surely I was losing my self-confidence, my joy in ministry, and my desire to be a pastor.

My wife's response was blunt: "Steve, put your resume together." Not only was she furious at the treatment I was receiving, but she was livid at the accusations made against our children. She was ready to pack our bags and leave on the next stage out of town.

I was emotionally overloaded, too stressed-out, and too demoralized to hear the truth of what she was saying. I stumbled on, hoping to find my way out of the war-zone that was now my church.

Now You See Him, Now You Don't

The situation between the board and me reached a stalemate. Though we all agreed we should work through the problem, the trust level had reached Depression Era lows.

In one last attempt to salvage the situation, I approached the leadership of a large and influential church that had ties to our congregation. I asked if they would be willing to act as mediators in the crisis. They readily agreed, and sent two men from their staff to begin meetings with the board and me.

My two critics wasted no time in listing their grievances. I didn't challenge their accusations, but opted instead to take an open and conciliatory stance. In front of everyone, I admitted I had mishandled the divorce controversy. I confessed that I had failed to follow their instructions on the matter. I asked for their forgiveness.

I hoped that by approaching the situation with humility and openness, it would draw a similar response from my antagonists. I was wrong.

When the mediators were through listening to everyone, they promised to return with their recommendations in a few days. I was hopeful the situation would now be resolved and I could get on with ministry.

But when they returned with their verdict, I was stunned. Siding with the board, they recommended I should immediately step down from the pulpit and take a forced leave of absence. Their decision was a hammer-blow.

When I regained my composure, I responded by saying, "Gentlemen, I don't think there's anything I could do in a reasonable period of time to rebuild trust. I've acknowledged my shortcomings, I've confessed my sins, and I've asked for forgiveness. I will honor your recommendation. But if we were going to turn a corner, I believe we would have done so long ago. Even with a sabbatical I don't sense there's any willingness to move on and rebuild the relationships."

What I was trying to say was that I knew from that moment on my ministry in the church was finished.

The next Sunday one of the board members stood before the congregation and simply announced I would be taking a leave of absence. No further explanations were offered. No questions from the members were allowed. One Sunday I was in the pulpit, the next Sunday I wasn't.

In the aftermath of the meeting, I weighed my options. None appeared good. Either I could try staying on at the church—which meant caving-in to the control of several men—or I could resign. Even if I did submit to the board, there was no guarantee I could stay on. They had already warned me that my reinstatement would require a long period of observation before making a decision about my future at the church.

It really didn't matter which way it went. By then my wife, my children, and I were exhausted. Our entire family was out of gas. Our desire to remain in the ministry was pointing toward empty.

The first Saturday of our sabbatical exemplified our brokenness. We were sitting in the living room when the terrible reality hit me. Turning to my wife I said, "Sandra, tomorrow's Sunday. Where are we going to go to church?"

We were two people without a country. Our forced exile had driven us from our spiritual home and family. We were no longer welcome among the people we had given our lives to for almost six years.

Together, we held each other and cried.

When individuals from the church would call and ask, "What's going on here?" all I could say was, "A situation has arisen between the board and me that we're trying to work through. If you want more specifics, call them."

I didn't want to leave myself open to the charge I was talking behind the board's back.

Those who did call the board for an explanation were given little information. They had decided as a matter of policy not to make any comment on the situation.

I would have had great difficulty coping with the stress if it weren't for the psalms. They were my life-line to God during those dark days. I grew in my empathy and understanding of David as I memorized large portions of the book.

My pain was sometimes so intense I would repeat a particular psalm at five-minute intervals throughout the entire day. That discipline kept me from giving in to an overpowering desire to hit back, or the urge to vindicate myself in the matter. Instead, I found the peace of mind to trust God for justice ultimately to prevail.

The Days After

As the sabbatical was nearing its end, I notified the board of my intention to resign. Their response surprised me. They asked me not to leave, which I thought strange, considering the unrelenting criticisms several had directed toward my ministry and character.

The mediators also cautioned me against leaving. But my family and I had had enough. We simply couldn't go on. I went ahead and gave official notice of my resignation.

In leaving I experienced the same emotions often felt at a funeral—loss, confusion, sorrow. Only in my case, no service was ever allowed for our friends and us to grieve. Though I had asked the board for an opportunity to share a farewell message with the congregation, they refused.

So, once again, I disappeared from the congregation with little or no explanation. The conclusion of my ministry at Brentwood was the equivalent of a private burial. By design of the board, it was closed-casket.

I lost more than a job. I had lost my place of worship, my friends, and my identity as a pastor all at once. It was a low point, perhaps the lowest, of my entire life.

Our first decision after resigning was to put our house on the market. It sold the first day. Knowing that our time in the area was coming to an end, I decided to lift the news black-out that had been in force during my sabbatical and resignation.

We met with close friends and supporters from the church and shared the story of our ordeal. I made an attempt to be as objective as I could about what had gone on. I admitted that I was partially to blame. I shared that I had blind-spots, weaknesses, and areas of needed growth in my life. I admitted I might have even sinned in failing to tell the divorced man everything the board had instructed me to.

But the one thing I couldn't bring myself to say was that I was a liar. Deep in my soul, I knew it wasn't so.

Too Conscientious to Object

Today I see more clearly the connection between the renewal of the church that was occurring, the winning of souls to Christ, and the rise of opposition to my ministry. But instead of seeing at the time the spiritual warfare that was happening, I took the route of blaming myself for the conflict. To a fault I gave credence to every charge and accusation made against me.

When criticisms were hurled at me, I uncritically accepted them reasoning, "This may be something God is trying to tell me." I didn't understand that other voices can sometimes sound so much like the voice of God.

Now that I had resigned, I was torn down the middle. I still loved people, loved the congregation, and loved God. But as far as I was concerned, I couldn't stand the local church. It was the pits.

Acting purely from a survival instinct, I determined never to place myself in a church setting where something like this could happen to me again.

Come Here, Go Away

My ambivalence toward the ministry became obvious in my search for a new job. Though I would send out my resume, as soon as I would receive a letter of interest, I trashed it. I did that for four months straight. I just couldn't bring myself to fill out a questionnaire or return a telephone call from any of the search committees.

Still smarting from the hurt I had received, I wasn't about to give anyone the right to scrutinize my life again. For a time I painted all church leaders with one broad brush: hyper-pious, judgmental, uncaring hypocrites.

God was continuing to work in my life, however. My first crucial step back toward ministry occurred one day when my father and I had a heart-to-heart conversation. We had moved in temporarily with my parents until we could locate new employment and housing.

Taking me aside, my father said, "Steve, I know you've been hurt badly by what's happened to you. But don't leave the ministry just yet. I believe God has his hand on you. Your gifts, education, and talents are too great to be discarded. Give it some more time before you make a final decision."

I had always respected my father. His advice that day seemed to touch a responsive chord in my heart, broken as it was. Though apprehensive and hurting, I decided to give God a few more weeks to change my mind. If nothing happened, I would call it a game in the ministry.

Taking Up Residence

It wasn't long afterward I was contacted by a close friend. He had a surprising proposal to make. His pastor, Dr. Bill Sullivan, was initiating a new program in their church known as the Pastor in Residence. The program was targeted at restoring to ministry pastors who were disillusioned and hurting because of a bad experience in the local church.

It seemed more than a coincidence. I indicated my openness to learning more, and within a few days Pastor Sullivan called and invited me to lunch.

Bill's easy-going, soft-spoken, and gentle manner immediately drew a response in my soul. His grandfatherly manner seemed to effortlessly coexist with his youthfulness and energy.

Over lunch I learned that his interest in wounded pastors was more than theoretical. He had twice left the ministry after difficult experiences in a parish. His spirit had been tenderized by those hard encounters. As we talked, I couldn't help but think of my father's prediction that God might still have a place for me in the ministry.

Besides wanting to empathize with hurting pastors, Bill had another motive in initiating this pilot program. It grew out of his one overriding conviction: a pastor is a terrible thing to waste.

It grieved him that crisis experiences, such as the one I endured, permanently drove so many ministers from the local church. He saw it as a tragic squandering of the resources of the kingdom of God.

He had done extensive research in exploring the reasons why pastors leave the ministry. His goal now was to find a way to stop the hemorrhage. He was determined to reclaim highly trained, competent, and caring individuals for the work of the local church.

After so many months of lying on the ecclesiastical road to Jericho, beaten and bleeding, I had at long last met a man willing to stop and pick me up. His invitation for me to enter the Pastor in Residence program was like oil poured on my wounds.

In nearly miraculous fashion, less than three months after I had left my church humiliated and bitter, I was preparing to reenter the ministry as a Pastor in Residence. I was by no means agreeing to accept another church if offered one. But I was taking the first step in that direction.

Preparing the Way Before Me

I was nervous about visiting Bill's church, Elim Community, for the first time. What would I say if people asked why I was here? Would I have to tell them about my past? Would I still be welcome if they knew the whole story?

Bill had anticipated those questions. He assured me he would make the proper introductions, explaining who I was, why I was here, and how long I would stay. If any contact had to be made with my prior church, he promised to be the liaison between the two groups.

I had expected a church initiating a Pastor in Residence program to be much larger. But on a good Sunday, Elim Community had no more than 150 in attendance. They didn't even own their own building; they met in rented facilities at the local elementary school.

I soon realized my initial fears were unjustified. The whole tenor of the church, including the worship service, was casual and easy-going, like Bill. After he introduced me that morning, the entire congregation broke into spontaneous applause. The sound of their clapping overwhelmed my soul. Fighting back tears, I just stood and absorbed the love and acceptance I had needed so badly. It was yet another significant healing moment in my journey back to ministry.

Bill did one more thing in preparing the way for me. He told the elder board they had only one responsibility toward me—to be my friend. I chose to share with them the circumstances behind my resignation from my former church.

I discovered how therapeutic it was to articulate my pain to a group of laymen who accepted me unconditionally. Most of them had come out of a church where they had witnessed conflict and infighting. They understood my sorrow, and without saying as much, gave me the permission to grieve in their presence.

'Tis a Gift to Be Simple, 'Tis a Gift to Be Free

The structure of the Pastor in Residence program was relatively simple. I was asked to make a six-month to one-year commitment to the church. In addition, I was instructed to raise my own financial support. Bill would assist me in sending out a fundraising letter to my friends and family. Finally, I would serve as a member of the staff and meet with Bill once a week.

Beyond that, I was not expected to carry any formal ministry responsibilities at the church. My time was my own. If I needed help or counseling in any area, the church promised to match me with the appropriate resources. I was free to do as much or as little as I wished.

Because I had previous training in Christian education, I began by assisting the Sunday school superintendent in arranging for classes and curriculum. Besides helping to keep me busy, it quietly reminded me that I still had something to offer the church.

I realized I needed to deal with the tremendous backlog of unresolved anger I carried from my previous church. Throwing resumes in the trash can was no long-term solution. I needed to face the rage boiling silently beneath the surface of my soul.

I sought the help of a person in the church finishing his master's degree in counseling at a local seminary. He graciously took me on without charge. Together with Bill's patient and wise counsel, the fiery outrage began to be extinguished.

The greatest hurdle of all was to forgive the men who had hurt me. It was a struggle to do so. Memories of their hurtful tactics returned again and again. But over time, as an act of my will, I began to let go of the bitterness. As I did, the chains of resentment began falling off. My understanding of Jesus' words to pardon someone seventy times seven took on special meaning. It was my duty to forgive my critics, even those who had called me a habitual liar.

A Heavy-weight Title

The Pastor in Residence program gave me back several things I had lost when I left Brentwood Community Church.

The first, and perhaps most important, was the sense of

integrity that goes with the title "pastor." When a pastor is stripped of his office and forced to pursue other work, he can face a credibility problem. If someone asks, "What are you currently doing?" it's awkward to respond by saying, "I'm selling insurance," or "I'm pumping gas," or "I don't have a job." It leaves you feeling like a fourteenth-round draft pick trying to make the team.

By assuming the title, "Pastor in Residence," I was able to negotiate with committees from a position of strength. I was a pastor applying for another pastorate, not a vocational outsider trying to get a foot in the door.

The second thing the Pastor in Residence program offered me was a safe place to sort out my feelings toward the ministry. Bill said, "Steve, I want to give you time to make a good decision about future local church ministry. Not one based on financial pressures, isolation, or a sense that no one cares."

That's exactly what the program provided. Our financial needs were met by sending out approximately forty letters with a cover letter from Bill. The church set a ceiling amount we could receive. The response was incredible. The support poured in. Each letter, each check, each note of encouragement was more than a financial gift. It was a vote I should stay in the ministry. Based on the outpouring of love we received, it took on landslide dimensions.

The gifts from Brentwood Church members meant the most to us. They were an affirmation that our ministry there had not been in vain. Since we had never had an official goodbye, it gave many people an opportunity to express their true feelings toward us.

The confirmation we experienced was more than financial. Elim Community also helped restore my self-esteem. Little by little, I quit berating myself over all that had gone on in my previous church.

While at Elim Community, people came alongside and said,

"Steve, you're a pastor. You have a pastor's heart. You can do it."
That helped me to begin to see myself as a pastor once again.
Little by little I was able to replace the negative messages I had
listened to with positive ones.

It was six months into the program when I first boarded a
plane for a job interview. Because of my unique role at Elim
Community Church, I was able to say to the committee, "I'll be
as open as you wish about my past situation. But if you feel you
need more information, call Bill Sullivan. He's knows the whole
story, and he'll be glad to discuss any aspect of it with you." With
nothing to hide and a strong reservoir of supporters back at the
church, my confidence levels were rising dramatically.

Though we didn't pursue that church any further, when we
arrived home and stepped off the plane, my wife and I looked at
each others and said, "We did it. We actually went and interviewed for a church."

I likened the experience to having a cast removed from your
arm after a football injury. Your first hit on the line tells you
whether or not you're back in the game. After that first interview,
I knew I was ready to play again. It felt good.

The final benefit of the Pastor in Residence program was the
opportunity for me to improve my conflict management skills.

One day I said to Bill, "I'm still an angry person. I believe
part of it is that I've never been taught how to resolve conflict. I
internalize problems and blame myself way too much."

Bill directed me to a series of tapes by the Alban Institute on
church conflict with material prepared by Norman Shawchuck. I
devoured the tapes. What was meant to take months to study, I
completed in a week. It helped me realize there are alternative ways
of dealing with conflict and each has its unique consequences.

When it came to church conflict, I had always flown by the
seat of my pants. But after my crash and burn, I was ready to
learn other methods.

The Wounded Healer

The day came when I was ready to leave the program. I accepted the call to my present church with newfound confidence and optimism.

About a year after I was settled in, I was troubled by the thought there might be other ministers out there who had left the ministry who needed the Pastor in Residence program. When I met a pastor in the area whose story sounded remarkably similar to my own experience at Brentwood, I knew it was time to repay the favor Bill had done me.

Not feeling the need to be original, I took Bill's ideas and implemented them here. Following his model, our Pastor in Residence program calls for a six-month to one-year commitment. It also requires a participant to raise his own support entirely from outside our church. The low-cost, highly personalized, easily adaptable nature of the program is its genius.

When a skeptical board member asks, "How much is this Pastor in Residence program going to set us back?" the answer is, "Not a penny."

And like Bill's program, there are no performance expectations placed on the individual. He can do as little or as much as he wishes. We make available a number of personality inventories and tests to help a person identify the emotional problems he may be struggling with. If he feels the need for a counselor, we make certain he is matched with a caring, competent therapist. In addition, we make retreat centers available to a husband and wife where they can be alone with God to sort out the big questions.

While you can't program love, you can communicate love through a program. That's what the Pastor in Residency does.

For example, one fascinating, unforeseen side-effect of the program is that we now have five former pastors in our congregation. The word has gotten out that we are a safe place for hurting ministers to hang out and recover. I'm delighted that we're seen as a secure haven.

Some time ago a man came to us who was nearly crucified in his former church because he changed his position from a four-point to a five-point Calvinist. When he shared with his church his doctrinal change of heart, he was told, "In three months you're out of here. You're done. That's it."

It took time for our board to learn why such experiences leave pastors devastated. Our board members are accustomed to the business world. There, losing and finding jobs is a way of life. No big deal. But I've helped them to see when a pastor loses his church, he loses more than a job. He loses his ministry, his identity, and his support system all at once. Our board members now have a real sensitivity and compassion for pastors who go through that awful experience.

My bottom line for continuing the program is this: it doesn't cost our church a dime to restore a pastor who has so much already invested in him. He is the product of literally thousands of dollars spent on education, years in training, and invaluable years of experience.

A *Christianity Today* Gallup poll once revealed that 30 percent of Protestant clergy think often about leaving the ministry. Bill Sullivan found in his doctoral research that 48 percent of those who do leave eventually want to return.

We've discovered it costs a church nothing but a heart of compassion to redeem individuals in whom God has invested so much. I too believe it is a terrible squandering of divine resources to waste a trained, gifted, and talented pastor. Sometimes it is the shepherd, not the sheep, who needs to be returned to the fold. When that happens, God is glorified, the church of Jesus Christ is expanded, and a valuable investment is redeemed.

When It's Time to Call 9-1-1

S ometimes congregations find themselves in a situation similar to what I faced the day I took my car to a local gas station to check the air pressure in my tires.

I pulled up to the air pump, parked my car, and got out. I
yanked the air hose to make it reach my car, and the nozzle blew
off the end like a rocket. I dropped the hose and it began whipping around like an angry rattlesnake as compressed air shot out
the end. I reached down and managed to pick it up, and looked
around for an attendant. A mechanic. Anybody who could help
me get control of this out-of-control situation. I had hold of
something I couldn't manage, and I had no idea what to do.

Churches often find themselves in the same predicament.
Conflict is escalating out of control, groups are taking sides, and
the church is in danger of splitting. It's time to call for help.

Two Bad Choices

The room was filled with an ugly tension. The elder board of
an East Coast church sat like a group of men on trial in front of a
badly divided congregation. Charges and counter charges flew for

most of the evening. At times, shouting erupted between members.

"Why don't we just admit we made a mistake when we called this man to be our pastor?" someone shouted.

"No we did not!" another person responded.

When a church reaches the place where it can no longer conduct its business or make decisions in a rational and caring manner, it often chooses between two less than desirable options: (1) fire the pastor, or (2) watch a sizable group of people head for the door.

In both scenarios, a divorce of sorts takes place. Relationships are severed, people move out, and everyone is left to try and pick up the pieces of a broken family.

Fortunately, there is a third option—to pick up the phone and call for help. For almost twenty-five years, two men with two very different backgrounds have been on the other end of the line. Their names are Norman Shawchuck and Speed Leas. They are church consultants who specialize in responding to calls from churches that are on the brink of dissolution or schism.

Why Not Just Punt the Pastor?

To many, the simplest and most obvious way to end a church conflict is to fire the minister. Once he's gone, so the conventional wisdom has it, everyone can get back to being one happy family.

Shawchuck strongly disagrees with that approach. "I don't readily buy the idea that the pastor is the cause of every church problem. Sometimes a collusion occurs between supervisory personnel and church boards. They decide that whenever a church gets into conflict the pastor should go. The problem is the pastor may go, but the church never resolves its conflict. The next pastor who arrives eventually gets caught up in the same unresolved disputes."

When Shawchuck is called to a church, he begins his work with a firm premise: "No one should leave. No lay people should leave, no clergy or staff should leave. We believe that if we can help people hang together long enough, we'll find a solution that satisfies everyone."

Speed Leas agrees. "You cannot work on systems or relationship issues by coming in and saying, 'Well let's see if we have enough evidence to get rid of the pastor.' I get impatient with people who say, 'Let's just figure out who the antagonistic lay people are and then fix this,' or 'Let's figure out who the crazy pastors are and get rid of them.' "

Building a Trust Fund

Like couples in a stormy and troubled marriage, churches often wait too long to seek help or counsel. By then, a significant amount of damage has been done. "By the time we arrive, the church has usually gone through at least one complete cycle or more of conflict—tension development to role dilemma to injustice collecting to confrontation to adjustment," Shawchuck says.

In those cases, conflict management consultants have to establish a beach head of trust with the pastor and congregation. "We go in with two objectives: (1) to create trust between the people and ourselves, and (2) to create trust in the process we're using even if the two sides can't trust each other. People want so much to get out of conflict that any sign of help coming reduces the tension. You have a window of opportunity," Shawchuck believes.

Sadly, things can get very ugly before help arrives on the scene. Shawchuck remembers one church on the verge of self-destruction. "Several years ago, I was called to a church of several thousand members. The pastor had been appointed against his will to serve this congregation. To make matters worse, the congregation had been virtually excluded from the selection process.

"It wasn't long until a mutual animosity, some would say hatred, developed between the pastor and the church. When a concerned member of the board finally contacted the denomination to tell them what was going on, he said, 'If you don't do something quickly, someone may be physically hurt.' " Shawchuck discovered he wasn't kidding.

"When I arrived I found tremendous anger on all sides. We were able to negotiate with the denominational leaders to have the pastor reappointed. When it was announced to the congregation the pastor would be leaving immediately, one member stood up and said, 'He can't leave. We aren't finished beating up on him yet.' "

It's Not Always as Bad as You Think

Couples in a troubled marriage often exaggerate problems. They just can't see anything good about their mate. But once some of their negative energy has been released, they began to see positive traits in the other person.

The same is true of churches. The level of conflict isn't always as bad as people believe. Sometimes they overestimate or exaggerate the problem. That's when a good conflict management consultant can help them see things in a more positive light.

"I try to help people evaluate the level of conflict they are at," says Leas. "Often, it's much lower than they believe it is. Some uncomfortable things were said at a public meeting in a church I'm working with at the present time. But when it was over, I said, 'Look, I hear objective statements being made. No one is universalizing or making radical demands. People are just saying what we should do differently. That's a healthy sign.' "

Restoring hope is also a key element in a successful conflict intervention. "We try to immediately demonstrate to the leaders and individuals involved in the conflict that we have ideas that will help. We try to engage people in talking about the problem in a nonthreatening way. As a rule, we start with the leadership team of the church. That way we learn about the situation while they release some of their negative energy," Leas says.

Getting People Back on Speaking Terms

In the best of all worlds, rational and reasonable people are willing to sit down and talk to one another in a rational and reasonable way. But conflict often produces irrational and unreasonable behavior. Just ask any marriage counselor. Or police officers called to the scene of a domestic argument. Or a church conflict management consultant.

When people have reached the place they will no longer speak to one another, a church conflict consultant has to get the process of communication started.

"I act as an interpreter when people won't sit in the same room with each other," says Leas. "Then I act as a mediator if I can get them in the same room. Often I'll paraphrase. For example, when someone says, 'You've never been responsible in your whole life,' I'll respond by saying, 'I think there probably are some areas where that person has been responsible. What you're talking about here is the irresponsibility of not showing up for work.'"

Shawchuck uses much the same approach. "If people are unable to communicate face to face, then we begin with private interviews. If some level of trust still exists, then we sit in and monitor their conversation. The final step is to go to larger group settings. They prove to be the most efficient means of settling a widespread conflict."

Sometimes the issue is not that people won't talk to one another, it's that others won't listen. Shawchuck remembers a serious incident where one group in a church simply was ignored in their cry for help.

"I once worked with a church of about 350 people. It was a long established church, but trouble soon developed among the younger couples. Several younger women charged that the pastor had made unwelcome sexual advances toward them."

When they brought their concerns to the selection committee who called the pastor, made up primarily of older individuals, they said, "No way. You're just trying to get at us by getting rid of the pastor."

"Not at all," the younger women said. "This is a dangerous situation. He has to go."

To make matters worse, the secretary filed suit against the church for sexual harassment. Everyone now was at loggerheads. The more established members continued to refuse to acknowledge a problem existed. They claimed the volunteer was lying. The official board seemed caught in the middle.

At that point, the church hired Shawchuck and an attorney to investigate. Shawchuck's first move was to contact the pastor's supervisor.

"How were things at this pastor's last church?" he asked.

"Fine, as far as we know," they said.

Shawchuck wasn't convinced, so he decided to contact the previous church directly.

"Why are you asking?" they said cautiously.

Shawchuck told them of the allegations against the pastor. Finally they admitted, "That's the same reason we asked him to leave."

Now armed with the evidence he needed, Shawchuck decided to meet directly with the older members and tell them the situation just as it was.

"I want you to stop this fight because you are wrong," he said. But Shawchuck wasn't prepared for their initial response.

"It doesn't matter," they replied. "This is our church, we're going to have it back our way."

With no further options available, Shawchuck decided to call a congregational meeting. Almost the entire church showed up.

"I asked the young women to tell their story," he remembers. "They did in detail. Then I asked the denominational executive to tell his story. He confirmed that the pastor had had similar problems at his previous church. After a few minutes of silence, several of the older members stood up and said, 'How come we didn't know this? We're sorry we didn't believe our younger women. What should we do?' "

"Now that you know the truth, get together and work through what you should do next," Shawchuck replied. The congregation voted to provide the pastor and his family a year's severance package. It was given on the condition that he agree to enter into therapy. The pastor consented and resigned his position.

But there was still one problem to be solved—the secretary's lawsuit against the church for sexual harassment. Shawchuck and the attorney met with her to discuss her legal action against the church.

"We apologize on behalf of the church for what happened to you," said Shawchuck.

"Is the pastor leaving?" she asked.

"Yes," she was assured.

"Is he going to get help?"

"Yes," we told her.

"Then I'll drop the lawsuit. It was never the money I wanted. I just wanted the church to be spared any further injury and for the pastor to get help."

By Faith Is a Church Saved

In the final analysis, it's not legal action or a well-timed intervention that puts a church back on the road to unity and health. It's the work of faith.

"It's faith that says, 'Okay, I'm going to try and connect with you and take you seriously. I'm going to believe that you are taking me seriously, as difficult as that might be to believe at the moment,' " according to Leas.

Once a church has taken the difficult steps of learning to trust and talk to one another again, there is still unfinished business to take care of—the difficult steps of offering forgiveness and being reconciled with former opponents. Again, the answer lies in the resources of faith.

"We provide for structured moments of reconciliation once the group is ready for that," says Shawchuck. "It usually takes six months to work up to that moment. It's often a time of silence with no words spoken.

"We use the Lord's Supper, which is a healing gift to the church. It brings people back to their faith. It causes them to think again about what they believe regarding confession, repentance, and God's ability to heal. In these moments of silence I've seen people kneel in front of someone, put their head on the floor, hug someone, shake hands, and weep. I've seen it all."

There is a reason why Shawchuck emphasizes silent reconciliation.

"In most instances people have already talked too much. Too many words have been thrown around. Besides, words always fail to fully express a moment of deep contrition. If we try to explain to someone how we feel, we move from our feelings back to our head. What saddens me is when the pastor refuses to participate in this time of contrition and reconciliation. When I see that happen, I know he won't be there for long."

Never Too Late to Apologize

Unfortunately, the pastor has sometimes left before the church calls 9-1-1. But even in those cases, as we've seen in previous chapters, it is still possible for restitution to take place.

"We once worked with a church that got into a horrendous fight. They really beat up the pastor and he left. Later, the church asked us to come and help them deal with what was going on in the parish. Eventually we brought the congregation to structured moments of confession and reconciliation with each other.

"Later, on their own, they realized that although they had been reconciled to each other, they had not been restored to their former pastor. So the board of elders wrote a twelve-page letter of confession and reconciliation. It was quite detailed. They mailed him the letter and waited for a reply.

"In about two months they got a letter back that said, 'I was healed by your letter. It was a real gift to me. When I left the church, I had decided to leave the ministry for good. Now I realize that the grace of God is still alive in the church. I've applied for appointment to another congregation.' Fortunately, I've seen that type of thing happen many times."

But what should you do when an individual or group has left the church? How much effort should a congregation make to bring expatriates back into the fold? When it comes to trying to coax groups back to the church, Leas is quite hesitant.

"I'm in favor of keeping the door open, but I'd be very cautious about taking back a group that has a leader. Once the pastor has left who prompted them to leave in the first place, people do return. But that needs to be a slow and careful process."

Spouse Abuse

Perhaps the most frequently overlooked, but most deeply wounded individual in a church conflict is the pastor's wife. She isn't given the benefit of sitting in on closed board meetings to express her thoughts or of speaking her heart from the pulpit. Shawchuck explains how she can be the victim of a cruel political game.

"All too often members who want to gripe about something, but don't have the guts to go directly to the pastor, will complain to his wife. They dump on her then walk away. They expect her to take the bad news back to her husband. In certain groups I've come to believe it's a cultural behavior. It's the acceptable way to get at pastors. I think it's wicked stuff."

That's why Shawchuck tries to offer special support to the pastor's spouse. "We allow her to be part of the entire conflict-resolution process. When I see a church abusing a pastor's spouse, I name it for what it is."

Same Old Song, New Lyrics

Both Leas and Shawchuck believe that the amount of conflict in the church has not changed much in the last three decades.

"I've been doing this for over twenty-five years and I can't tell the difference," Leas says. "It doesn't feel any different as far as the issues people fight over or the way they behave. People do seem more accepting of turning to outside consultants for help."

Shawchuck agrees, but sees some ominous trends at work. "I don't believe there is more conflict today, but I do believe today's conflicts are more difficult, damaging, and complex than they were twenty years ago. When I started in this work, people in serious conflict usually wanted to get it together. Today, they aren't as willing to reconcile. People tend to be intransigent, unwilling to listen."

A newer trend that complicates the matter of bringing healing and unity to a local church is the breakdown of families in our culture.

"There is more dysfunction in congregations than twenty years ago," says Shawchuck. "I believe this may be a reflection of our society. As divorce escalates and more children are living in broken homes, people bring that hurt with them. The congregation becomes a reflection of individual brokenness. Many of the churches we work with are clinically dysfunctional."

He believes dysfunctional congregations tend to choose a dysfunctional pastor. "I believe they can find a dysfunctional pastor two thousand miles away. They need a codependent person or identified patient to use to expunge their guilt. Regardless of how sick a group might be, they often take comfort in the fact that someone in their group is worse off than they are. That's the role the identified patient plays out. It helps him or her feel like a martyr. They feel good they can suffer for the people. It reinforces their sense of a lack of self-worth."

Yeah, but Does It Work?

When all is said and done, when can calling 9-1-1 be considered a success? Leas looks for several signs of health to reappear.

"Tension is reduced. Clear decisions are made. The church now has the ability to manage future problems." Leas evaluates his work by contacting various leaders in the church to get their assessment of the progress that's been made. He makes a distinction between healing and crisis intervention.

"Intervention is simply stopping some sort of bizarre action or making a decision. But establishing healthy patterns is far more difficult. It often takes nine to twelve months of working with a church to work on those kinds of relationships."

Often the results are encouraging.

"In 42 percent of the cases, significant progress was made on all the goals we set out to achieve," Leas says. "In 29 percent of the cases, some progress has been made on some of the goals, but not on all of them. In 23 percent, things didn't get any better, but neither did they get any worse. And in 6 percent of the cases, things got worse during the consultation. In those cases it usually ends up in an ecclesiastical or secular court, or a significant group in the church leaves."

Conclusion

It's not a sign of weakness but of wisdom when a group knows it's time to call for outside help. Like most emergencies, time is of the essence. Waiting too long can be catastrophic. But if a church receives the attention and help it needs in a timely manner, it stands a good chance of full recovery.

CHAPTER 13

Taming Your Animal Instincts

A church that manages conflict well is simply a collection of individuals who have learned to manage it well.

Each of us has learned our own method for dealing with conflict. Some of us dig in our heels and fight, while others turn tail and head for the hills. In this fictional account of a divided women's group in a church, the five most common ways people react to conflict are illustrated. Perhaps you will recognize yourself in one of these characters.

Fortunately, just as we learn negative ways of dealing with conflict, so we can also learn more productive methods.

"If the church won't provide paid baby-sitters for the Friday Bible study, I won't be coming back," Susan said, her voice trembling with anger. "I don't need to spend my Friday morning in a nursery changing diapers and holding crying babies when I can do that at home. I come here for a break, not more work. And I'm not the only one who feels this way. There are other young mothers besides me who are planning to quit the Bible study unless the church begins paying for childcare."

Helen, an older woman on the board who sat across from Susan, was carefully devising a compromise plan to avoid a split between the older and younger women.

"Susan," she said, "I think I understand why some of the older women oppose paying baby-sitters. When I was your age we all took turns in the nursery on Friday mornings. None of us expected a free ride. While I don't necessarily agree with them, some feel your generation doesn't seem willing to make sacrifices. But I'll tell you what, why don't the mothers care for the nursery one week, and the other week we'll pay for childcare from our Friday Bible study dues."

Susan, undaunted, pressed the attack. "That's not good enough," she said firmly. "It's fully funded childcare every Friday or we walk."

Denise was desperately looking for a way to bring this threatening confrontation to a quick end. "I think we should drop the whole issue and plan our fall retreat," she said nervously. "We're all believers and we shouldn't be arguing like this. Someone will end up getting hurt." The group stared at her for a moment, then went on with the debate.

"Excuse me," Denise whispered. "I just remembered my son forgot his lunch at home today." With that she exited the room, avoiding eye contact with anyone.

Iola, an elderly woman, was something of a nurturing mother to everyone in the church. Her empathy, kindness, and unselfishness brought comfort and encouragement to countless individuals. She hated disagreements of any kind and worked hard to stop them before they got started.

"I think this whole problem is my fault," she said with sincerity. "When I was president last year I forgot to set enough aside to help with baby-sitting. But I have a little nest egg at home that would take care of paying sitters for the remainder of the year. Let's tell the young mothers the problem is resolved."

The group knew Iola lived on a fixed income and couldn't afford such a gesture. Susan and Helen both agreed letting Iola pick up the tab wasn't the answer.

Eunice, the pastor's wife, was the last to speak.

"I believe there's a way to solve this problem, but it isn't by forcing a vote on the matter today. This isn't a battle to be won or lost, it's a problem to be solved. I think we need to reexamine the goals of the Friday morning Bible study, and then openly discuss the impact our current policies are having on our relationships. This may take some time to resolve, but I think we'll be a stronger group when we've finished the process."

Seated at the end of the linen-covered table was Alice, the current president of the Women's Ministries. Who should she listen to? What should she do next? Would this issue divide the group?

Instincts for Survival

A conflict management specialist would advise Alice to consider the survival instincts manifested in each woman's advice. Borrowing from the names of various animals frequently associated with certain types of behavior—from aggressive confrontation to complete avoidance. Susan would be considered a shark, Helen a fox, Denise a turtle, Iola a teddy bear, and Eunice an owl. Perhaps a case could be made that the board meeting was less a routine business session and more a scene from Mutual of Omaha's *Wild Kingdom*.

Actually no physical metamorphosis had taken place, but each woman revealed her conflict management survival instincts in the discussion. Each was acting to try to reduce the tensions she was experiencing.

Tension develops whenever one person or group is threatened by the actions of another person or group. The threat may be against one's person (or psyche), position, power, or status. In conflict situations, people instinctively act to protect their perceived "territory" in the group. In this case, control of the Bible study and its finances were the disputed Falkland Islands. The younger women demanded paid childcare; the older women deemed it a waste of resources. Each group was attempting to preserve its own turf.

Because the main concern of a living organism is survival, humans like animals, develop certain responses to threatening situations. But unlike animals, humans are uniquely gifted with the ability to observe, act, and reflect on their own conduct. People alone have the capacity to alter their behavior.

Along with the five different responses to conflict come five potentially different results. The different outcomes include a win-lose, win-a-little lose-a-little, lose-lose, lose-win, and win-win resolution to the conflict. Let's examine each one in more detail.

Fins in the Baptistery

Sharks are competitors by nature. They see the entire world in terms of win or lose. They tend to be domineering, aggressive, and open to any solution as long as it's the one they want. Because winning is the ultimate goal, sharks tend to do whatever it takes to prevail. They'll use persuasion, power plays, and coercion as need be. Sharks don't always appear menacing and may even possess a quiet demeanor. But make no mistake, they always play to win.

Susan had probably learned early in her life that acting as a shark was the most effective way to help her survive threatening situations at home, at school, or in the neighbor's backyard. She took that preferred method of dealing with conflict into adulthood. Though she lacked gray skin and three rows of teeth, she still approached the baby-sitting brouhaha in Jaws-like fashion.

Her threat to lead a walk-out of the young mothers was a classic shark tactic. Either she and her friends would get their way, or they would fold their chairs in the Friday morning Bible study. Typical of a shark, she was going for a win at all costs.

There are dangers in always giving sharks their way. When win-lose individuals are allowed to rule the church, subsurface anger can begin to build, people can feel coerced, and a dangerous dependency can grow up around the strong-willed person. A good rule of thumb: When you seen an ominous fin circling in the baptistery, don't climb in.

Foxes in the Vineyard

Helen, on the other hand, was not a competitor but a compromiser. Typical of the fox, she hoped to slice the pie in such a way that everyone believed they got the biggest slice. Foxes always look to cut a deal.

Helen's suggestion that they split the cost of childcare between the young mothers and the deacons was her attempt to help everyone win-a-little, lose-a-little. She was sincere in her desire to keep the group from splitting.

Unfortunately, compromise has a bad name in the church. It's used in some circles as a synonym for worldliness or moral laxity. But in organizational terms, a compromiser is a person sincerely working to keep a group from breaking apart, who uses bargaining and conciliation to prevent it from happening.

Foxes are usually flexible people, and their primary interest is in achieving the common good. If people don't immediately respond to their suggested bargain, they aren't above using persuasion, arm-twisting, and manipulation to force an agreement if necessary. Helen planned to do a good deal of behind-the-scenes negotiating to persuade both parties to accept her solution.

There are times when a split-the-difference approach is a sensible way of solving minor disputes. If one group wants to serve dill pickles and the other sweet, why not put out two dishes?

But compromise is not always the answer. It can send people away half-satisfied and half-committed to the solution. In that case, the problem will emerge again later in a different shape or size.

Before we judge the fox or any of the other styles too harshly, it's helpful to remind ourselves that each person chooses a style to help them survive in a highly stressful situation.

Helen sincerely believed she was representing the interests of both parties in the dispute. But her solution didn't address the underlying issues of ownership and control. Even if her compromise proposal had been accepted, these issues would inevitably reemerge at a later time.

Avoidance in a Half-Shell

Denise had grown up in an abusive home. She now was a young mother herself and secretly favored subsidized childcare, but she was afraid to say so. She had learned as a young girl that when others fight, she got hurt. And if she happened to disagree and said so, she got hurt even more. Her response to every threatening situation was to avoid the problem at all costs. Denise had become a turtle.

Turtles are so frightened by conflict that their solution to any problem is to avoid it all together. They favor a lose-lose solution to every confrontation. They honestly believe that a world without conflict is the only one they can survive in, so they flee the scene of any altercation. Some actually get up and walk-out as Denise did, while others simply withdraw into a state of emotional neutrality and numbness.

Because turtles so intensely dislike conflict, they are often mistaken for peacemakers in the church. Actually, they are peacekeepers, and there's a profound difference. By attempting to preserve the peace by denying or avoiding all thorny issues in the church, they unwittingly set up the church for major problems.

When Denise suggested they drop the subject of baby-sitters and discuss something else, she was leaving the childcare problem for others to deal with. She was unwilling to play any part in the needed process of conflict resolution: cooperation in defining the conflict, mutual involvement in seeking a solution, and working together to implement an agreement once a consensus is reached.

There are moments when avoiding a conflict altogether makes sense. Proverbs reminds us it is the glory of a person to overlook an insult (19:11). We ought to choose carefully which hills we are willing to die on. Some battles just aren't worth fighting. Why not just agree to respect each other's viewpoint? Is it worth breaking fellowship over?

But avoidance as a long-term strategy for coping with serious conflict simply won't work. Denial won't bring peace and reconciliation to a group struggling with burning internal issues.

Turtles, while appearing to be peaceable and gentle souls, often are hiding a great reservoir of hidden anger, frustration, and deep-seated hostility. Denise, while on the surface appearing to be calm and sedate, struggled with unresolved rage and bitterness toward her parents. She never felt the freedom or confidence to confront her abusive past, and carried the resentment from it like hidden molten lava in her soul.

Turtles face such emotional pain as the result of years of avoiding the unhappy task of dealing with conflict on the job, in their families, or in the church. They pay a high price for sweeping everything under their emotional carpet.

Warm and Fuzzy Accommodation

Iola's willingness to pay for the baby-sitting herself, or blame herself for the controversy, is typical of the most lovable of all creatures in the conflict management menagerie—the teddy bear.

The teddy bear readily surrenders his or her own interests or goals in a threatening situation to accommodate the interests or goals of the disagreeing party. Iola never expressed her opinion on the childcare issue, but immediately attempted to placate Susan and the other young mothers. There is a sense in which teddy bears will try to maintain peace at any price.

Like the turtle, the teddy bear will attempt to steer the group away from any controversial issues. But failing that, they try another tactic to defuse the situation. They switch to showing increased personal concern for the others, working hard to create a more relaxed, easy-going, or loving atmosphere.

Bless her heart, who could fault Iola for trying to solve the dilemma by paying for the childcare herself? She was simply trying to keep the opposing parties apart. Her display of concern for both sides of the issue was commendable. That's why teddy bears are often seen as super-spiritual people in dealing with conflict. In true sacrificial fashion, they attempt to atone for the problem by bearing it themselves.

There is an up side to using accommodation to solve a conflict. The willingness to surrender our selfish interests or goals in pursuit of peace in the family or church is often a sign of godliness and maturity. If someone really wants roast beef rather than turkey served at the Christmas luncheon, even though my diet won't allow it, it's not worth dividing the group over. I'll bring my own lunch and microwave it.

So was it wrong for Susan and the young mothers to express their needs? Was it wrong for the older women to bring up their financial concerns? No. Both were expressing legitimate points of view.

But Iola believed that relationships take priority over any issue, and therefore any contention that might divide people was wrong. What Iola failed to see is that the long-term impact of constantly acting as an accommodator in conflict settings is less than desirable.

Teddy bears unknowingly give the victors in a conflict an unreal sense of their own rightness. On a personal level, though they appear cheerful and easy-going, accommodators can often struggle with a sense of falsehood. They have surrendered their personhood so often they aren't sure they are a person any longer. The emotional price of furiously trying to keep relationships together takes its toll on them as well.

No one knew it, but Iola was tired of trying to keep the Friday Bible study together, and had plans to quit in the spring.

Spotting the Collaborative Owl

Eunice alone saw the baby-sitting controversy as a problem to be solved, not as a battle to be won. Her desire was to see everyone leave the table with a win-win solution. Her insistence that the group reevaluate the goals of the Bible study, and then assess the impact the current policies were having on relationships between older and younger women, is typical of the collaborator.

Collaborators are individuals who "colabor" with all the parties involved until a mutually satisfying solution is found. Their strength lies in their willingness to stay with a task or problem until it's solved.

Another asset collaborators bring to a conflict situation is their perspective on the problem. They see a dispute as an opportunity to strengthen a group, not destroy it. Eunice wasn't afraid of the childcare issue. She recognized that it was symptomatic of the generational differences in the group. She saw it as an opportunity to address the larger issue of how the older and younger women were going to share control and ownership of the Bible study.

Eunice's goal was not to overcome or avoid the differing adversaries, but to engage them both in constructive dialogue. Here's how she eventually helped the group solve the childcare dilemma.

First, she generated as much valid and useful information as possible. Eunice arranged for a meeting with a representative group of young mothers and older women. She asked the young mothers why paid childcare was so important to them. As they explained their busy schedules, including part-time jobs to help make ends meet, the older women were surprised to learn how stressful their lives actually were.

As Susan explained how her newborn seldom slept entire nights, they could see that exhaustion, not laziness, was behind her request to be relieved of baby-sitting duties.

As the younger women heard the older ladies, several of whom were widows, explain their difficulties in living on fixed incomes, they realized several could not afford higher dues to pay for childcare. They assumed it would be expensive.

Through the dialogue, both groups learned that the other brought different needs and expectations to the study. The younger women were looking for a rest, the older women for companionship. As a result, misconceptions, false assumptions, and wrong conclusions about each other were filtered out of the discussion. The group took a significant step toward long-term peace when they acknowledged the younger women weren't lazy, they were exhausted, and the older women weren't greedy, they were living with serious financial constraints.

The next step was to help the entire group make free and informed choices about a future course of action. Eunice helped both sides to see where they were in agreement and where they weren't. To their amazement, the group realized how much they actually agreed on. Everyone felt it was a benefit to have both older and younger women participate. They all believed that sharing their struggles and praying together helped them cope with the problems they faced. And they all agreed they didn't want the group to split in two over the childcare issue.

While there was a consensus that the economic burden of childcare needed to be distributed, the group still differed over how it should be done. Some continued to support the every-other-week plan, while others wanted weekly subsidized childcare.

The final step was to bring everyone into the decision-making process and motivate them to be personally committed to the final agreement. Eunice, the owl, was wise enough to realize that people tend to support solutions they help create. After a lengthy period of brainstorming ideas of how to fund the childcare, some-one suggested that they hold a fundraiser to generate funds for a year's worth of baby-sitting.

They decided on a holiday boutique sale. Several of the older women agreed to make quilts, which typically sold for several hundred dollars in retail shops. The added benefit of the project was companionship—they could work on them together. It would also help fill up some of the empty time during the holiday seasons when loneliness was particularly a problem.

As for the younger women, several ran home-based computer businesses and agreed to work on mailing lists and publicity. Two of the younger women also had artistic talents in watercolor and pottery, and agreed to sell some of their work at the boutique and donate the profits to the project.

As a result, the Women's Ministries held the most successful fundraising event in the history of the church. And they grew closer to one another. Though the millennium didn't arrive, the shark, the fox, the turtle, the teddy bear, and the owl did learn to live with one another. The Wild Kingdom had been tamed.

This article originally appeared in *Leadership Journal* 14 (Winter 1993) under the title, "Animal Instincts: Five Ways Church Members Will React in a Fight," by Robert Moeller and Norman Shawchuck.

CHAPTER 14

On Earth as It Is in Heaven

The voice on the other end of the phone was weak and raspy. I had to strain to hear what he was saying, "Goodbye, Bob. I'll see you again."

Those were the final words of a dear friend of mine, a former seminary president, from his hospital bed shortly before he died of cancer.

I wept as I put down the receiver that day. We both knew we would never talk with each other in this life. But we both drew comfort in another fact. Someday, we would see each other again face to face. We both belonged to the church of Jesus Christ, so we knew we would one day walk the streets of heaven together.

The promise of heaven and the pain of earth intersect in the life of every believer. In the local church, both eternity and time meet in the pews. The people we sit next to on Sunday morning are the very people, in most instances, that we will spend forever with.

Because we share an eternal relationship with other believers, it makes sense we learn to solve our differences and conflicts here and now. It's the Father's will that we love one another on earth as we shall in heaven.

A Head Start on Paradise

I grew up in an exciting, sometimes tumultuous, multiracial church. It was a continual challenge for all of us, regardless of our race, to overcome our natural apprehensions and suspicions of one another. Our culture had taught us to believe something that wasn't true. Namely, there is more that divides us than we have in common. For Christians, nothing could be further from the truth.

However imperfectly, we managed to learn to love and accept one another in that church. One of the black leaders in the congregation said it best: "We're going to be spending eternity together, so we might as well learn how to get along with each other down here."

I believe working out our relationships in the local church is part of God's plan for each of us. If God had wished to do so, he could have taken us into heaven the moment we became a believer. Like Enoch in the Old Testament, we could have walked directly into the presence of God.

But God, in his infinite wisdom, chose to leave us on earth, to live out the remainder of our lives in an imperfect, sinful world. He decided to let our character develop and expand by placing us in the local church with other imperfect, sometimes sinful human beings like ourselves.

Why does God bring two different people together in a church? To argue? To question each other's motives? To get on each other's nerves?

No, God's purpose is to teach us what heaven is like.

Heaven is a place where people who are very different in their backgrounds, temperaments, and even convictions on some issues are going to sit across the table from one another. The common denominator will be that each resident of Paradise will have been saved, by grace, through faith, in the finished work of Christ.

In heaven, the arguments we had on earth about any number of nonessential matters, some of which led to serious conflict and division, will suddenly be put in their proper perspective. It will be like going up fifty stories and looking down from the top of a tall building. The trucks, cars, and masses of people that seemed so large on the street will now look far less significant from such a high vantage point.

Both Martin Luther and John Zwingli agreed that salvation was a work of grace through faith, and not a result of any work or act that we might perform. They both believed it was the death and resurrection of Christ that had purchased their salvation.

Yet these two giants in the Reformation could not see eye to eye on the meaning of the Lord's Supper. The one, and perhaps only time they met to discuss their theological differences, they got into a serious argument.

Reportedly, Luther had anticipated their differences over the nature of communion, and had written the German word *ist* (which means "is" in English) in chalk on the table. He then covered it with a tablecloth. When Zwingli arrived and challenged him to show him one word in the New Testament to prove his theory of the Lord's Supper, Luther reportedly ripped off the tablecloth and pointed to the *ist* and said, "This is my body..."

The two were unable to come to an agreement that day, and a major division among Protestants resulted. Now the meaning of the Lord's Supper is a significant issue. But neither man believed it was a means of salvation. They both knew they would meet in heaven despite their differences.

Theologians obviously differ as to who was right and who was wrong in that interchange, depending on their own theological convictions. But isn't it remarkable that one word kept two men apart who had so much else in common?

As large as the word *ist* appeared to the both of them on earth, I imagine in heaven, basking in the light of God's eternal glory, it now appears in somewhat smaller letters. While it's possible one was completely correct and the other completely incorrect, I imagine both of them now realize that they both saw somewhat "through a glass darkly."

Regardless of our differences over matters that aren't essential to salvation, it is God's will that believers maintain a spirit of humility and love toward one another. It is also his will that we work together, without surrendering our individual distinctives or convictions, to fulfill his command to share the Good News of Christ with every person on earth. Paul put it this way to the church at Philippi:

> If you have any encouragement from being united with Christ, if any comfort from his love, if any fellowship with the Spirit, if any tenderness and compassion, then make my joy complete by being like-minded, having the same love, being one in spirit and purpose. Do nothing out of selfish ambition or vain conceit, but in humility consider others better than yourselves (Phil. 2:1-3).

If there is any common basis we share as a result of our common salvation experience, if the Holy Spirit is at all at work drawing us toward one another, if we have any love and concern for one another, then let that be the basis for unity and harmony among us.

It's possible to be like-minded (literally "in harmony of mind") without agreeing on every issue concerning the Christian life. What's vital is the spirit in which we discuss these matters and even disagree with one another.

As Bill Hybels says, "I can have a rough-and-tumble leadership meeting with someone, but because we're committed to community, we can still leave, slapping each other on the back, saying, 'I'm glad we're still brothers.' We know no one's bailing out just because of a conflicting position. Community is bigger than that."[1]

The Four Spiritual Laws of Building Unity

When it gets right down to it, we either believe that the unity Paul is talking about is possible in the local church, or it's fantasy. Either God intended the church to be a place of harmony and oneness of spirit and purpose, or it's just wishful thinking. I'm of the opinion God is serious in his desire to see love in action among believers.

But what steps are necessary for this to occur? Let me suggest four commitments each member of a local body of believers must make to see love in action released in their congregation. Each step calls not only for belief, but for response as well. It does no good to say we believe in the laws of aerodynamics if we refuse to set foot on an airplane. We need to take steps to prove we mean what we say.

1. Believe and act as if you have far more in common with other believers than what divides you.

I remember standing in the cold drizzle of a January rain in London one New Year's Eve. I was a visiting college student on a study tour. Because it was New Year's Eve none of the cabbies wanted to venture into our part of London. There were loud parties and rowdy celebrations going on all around me. So I stood and shivered along with dozens of other hapless travelers outside the train station.

Then I heard two women behind me who sounded like they were Americans. One left the line to go search for a taxi further from the station. Minutes later, a black sedan pulled up, and the woman flung open the door. She motioned for her friend to join her, and I saw my chance. I picked up my bags, ran toward the taxi and yelled, "I'm an American too. Can I ride with you?"

"Sure, get in," they yelled back.

Once safely inside the cab and away from the noise and confusion on the streets, I introduced myself.

"Where are you from?" one of the women asked.

"I'm from Minneapolis. How about you?"

They looked at one another in surprise. "We're from Fridley" (a suburb just to the north of Minneapolis). We all laughed. Thousands of miles from home, in a strange and foreign city, in the midst of a wild and tumultuous celebration, we suddenly discovered just how close we were to each other.

As Christians, we are still far from home. We live as aliens and strangers in a foreign city, in the midst of turbulent times. But we are closer to one another than we think. We share the same eternal Word of God, the same promise of eternal life, and the same indwelling Holy Spirit. All that far outweighs whatever personality, political, and preference differences we might have with one another.

Paul reminds us, "For we were all baptized by one Spirit into one body—whether Jews or Greeks, slave or free—and we were all given the one Spirit to drink" (1 Cor. 12:13).

Often it takes persecution and pressure for us to realize our common bonds. The testimony of believers in other lands who have gone through times of testing and outright opposition confirms this. Under pressure, Christians suddenly discover how precious their like faith is.

Chuck Colson tells the story of Aleksandr Solzhenitsyn and his time as a prisoner in Russia. One day, when his strength had given out, he sat down on a bench. The usual penalty for such an unauthorized break from the regimen of forced labor was a shovel across the head.

That day, Solzhenitsyn didn't care; he would rather die than go on.

Another prisoner, sensing what was about to happen, walked

over and sat down next to the great Russian writer. In the dirt in front of him he drew an image of the Cross. The two men looked at one another, and suddenly Solzhenitsyn realized he had found a brother in Christ. The presence of that believer in the midst of the horror of the gulag gave him new courage. He was able to get up and resume his work.

It's doubtful Solzhenitsyn ever learned that man's denominational affiliation, but it didn't matter. He was a fellow Christian, and that was far more important than whatever else might have separated them.

For unity to live and prosper in the local church, we must believe we are more like one another than we are different. From God's point of view, we belong to one another not only for this life, but for the one to come as well.

2. Believe and act as if God has a purpose for bringing us together in the local church.

As ornery, difficult, and stubborn-minded as other people might be, if they too have placed their faith in Christ alone for their salvation, they are part of our family. As a professor of mine used to say, "We inherit our brothers and sisters, we don't choose them."

Just as God had a purpose in mind when he allowed us to be born into our family of origin, God has a purpose in placing us in the midst of other believers. "Now you are the body of Christ, and each one of you is a part of it" (1 Cor. 12:27).

One of my happiest and most fulfilling experiences in ministry occurred almost by accident. A church called and asked if I could fill in for one Sunday in June. I was working full-time at a college and seminary, so I wasn't looking to assume another pastorate.

But I agreed to go for one Sunday, and on that day, we were invited out to lunch to discuss the church's needs. Because we had several small children with us, I declined the offer. But when I got into the car and told my kids we had been invited to a nice restaurant but had turned it down, a small rebellion erupted.

"You what!" they cried in unison. "Please, Dad, can't we go?"

I relented, but our hosts had already left the church. We pulled out onto a busy city street and started home.

"There they are!" shouted my oldest son, Rob. He was right. We drove up next to them at a stoplight and motioned for them to roll down their window.

"We'd like to eat lunch with you," I shouted over the traffic. They looked somewhat bewildered, but nodded yes. That lunch led to a two year interim pastorate that God used in my life in a significant number of ways. God had a purpose for our coming together, and now I see that it was no accident God led us to that church for the time he did.

For reasons you may not fully understand, God places you with other believers who are different from you. But whether it is to teach us patience, encourage our spirits, or help us learn to agree to disagree, God is at work. In fact, if you find yourself at a church where everyone thinks and acts exactly alike, chances are you won't grow much there.

3. Believe and act as if love is the most excellent way of living and worshiping together.

Several years ago there was an improbable game show known as *The Gong Show*. Amateur talent would perform before a supposed panel of critics. The panelists would rate the individual performers on their talent, style, and overall performance. Every so often an act would appear that was such a disaster, one of the panelists would take a giant mallet and whack a gong with it. It was the ultimate statement of ridicule. It meant that the performance was just too painful to continue to listen to.

Paul said it was possible for a believer to possess certain

spiritual gifts, but if that person practices his gift without love toward others, he is "only a resounding gong or a clanging cymbal" (1 Cor. 13:1).

Churches can perform well in a number of areas, such as music, preaching, education, outreach, and missions, and still lack love. Paul says you can excel in all these ministries but if you don't practice love for one another, you gain nothing, you are nothing. That's tough language, but when you consider it, it makes sense.

Love is an essential character trait of God. When a person, or a church, fails to show love, it is a denial of the person of God. The apostle John says, "Whoever does not love does not know God, because God is love.... No one has ever seen God; but if we love one another, God lives in us and his love is made complete in us" (1 John 4:8,12).

There are numerous ways to organize a congregation, there are a variety of worship styles that can be used, and literally hundreds of ways to design a church building. But the most excellent way for a local church to follow is the way of love.

Love helps you forgive the person who made a thoughtless remark about you in a board meeting. Love allows you to look past a person's irritating voice or bad habit of interrupting you. Love allows you to accept a person's eccentric behavior. Love covers a multitude of sins.

I've learned to brace myself when someone says, "Bob, may I be honest with you?" Usually I'm about to absorb a zinger. One day a man looked at me and said, "I don't like your glasses. They look like goggles." The person who said that had given a majority of his adult life ministering to others in a difficult situation. I couldn't take offense at his remark. The love and respect I have for him and his wife wouldn't allow me to. (Later I did get new glasses and I did look better.)

There are situations where I have had to go back and share

the hurt someone's remark has left on me. But even in those cases, it's love that allows me to give and receive forgiveness.

Love is what makes you credible to the outside community. I remember a man who visited our clothing distribution center one winter morning. He was nearly beside himself with joy. He had found a pair of shoes that fit him. Only later did I learn he worked at a local car wash, where his feet got wet during the day. Walking home after work each night, his shoes would freeze solid in the frigid northern climate. Now he would have a dry pair of shoes for the walk home.

He could have cared less whether we sang hymns or choruses, had a Saturday evening or Sunday evening service, or whether we raised hands or kept them by our sides during worship. He had found a church that cared if his feet were dry in ten degree weather.

A chemist friend once said that water is the universal solvent. If that's true in the physical world, then love is the universal solvent in the spiritual world. It dissolves and absorbs a host of toxic attitudes, behaviors, and prejudices among believers. It is the more excellent way.

4. *Believe and act on the knowledge that Jesus is Lord of the church. It belongs to him, not us.*

Shortly after we were married, Cheryl and I agreed to house-sit for friends of ours. Even though they had given us the freedom to use the kitchen, relax in their living room, and come and go as we pleased, we were conscious that it was their house, not ours. We didn't track mud onto the carpet, we didn't leave dirty dishes in the sink, nor did we invite a hundred people over for an all-day party on their lawn. It would have been wrong to act as if it were home when it wasn't. We had been left in charge to care for the residence, not abuse it. We knew that one day the rightful owners would return, and we would have to given an account of the condition of their house.

The same is true of Christians in the local church. One day our Lord and Savior is coming back. When he does, we will have to give an account of how we treated his precious possession, the church.

Like the fictitious story of "The Dig" earlier in the book, what will later generations find when they sift through the remains of the church we leave? Will it be a legacy of infighting and division, or will there be evidence that we loved and worked together for the sake of the gospel?

It's important to stop and ask ourselves some crucial questions before we do or say something that will damage the unity of the local church:

Will my anger accomplish the righteousness of God, or will it given Satan a foothold in our congregation?

Do I truly have the good of everyone involved in mind, or am I acting out of selfish ambition?

Is it my love for God or my wounded ego that's driving me to criticize and denounce another believer?

Is my motive to see a fallen brother or sister restored or to see them punished and humiliated?

Am I upholding biblical standards or have I set myself up as someone else's judge and jury?

Will my resigning and leaving solve the problem or create a larger problem?

If the church is truly God's possession and not our own, we must be careful how we handle it. It has been purchased with the very blood of Jesus Christ. Any item that valuable demands we do all we can to preserve, protect, and safeguard it from fissure or cracks. Like guards who subdued the terrorist who tried to smash one of Michelangelo's sculptures, we should be on guard against those who would hammer away at the priceless unity of the local church.

To preserve the unity and harmony of the church we must not only take the four steps I've outlined, but we must remain vigilant. Peter warns us that our adversary is like a roaring lion, who prowls about seeking people (and churches) he may destroy (1 Pet. 5:8). If we don't actively pursue peace, and remain on guard against conflicts that could destroy our unity, we may wake up one morning and find the church in shambles.

The January 13, 1992, issue of *Fortune* magazine featured the "Biggest Goofs of 1991."

In an act of corporate cooperation, AT&T reached an agreement with the power company in New York City, Consolidated Edison. The contract stated that whenever power demands exceeded the utility's grid, AT&T would lessen their demands on the electric utility by throwing a switch, unplugging some of its facilities, and drawing power from internal generators at its 33 Thomas Street station in lower Manhattan.

On September 17, AT&T acted in accordance with their agreement. But when AT&T's own generators kicked in, the power surge kicked out some of their vital rectifiers (circuit boards), which handled 4.5 million domestic calls, 470,000 international calls, 1,174 flights across the nation carrying 85,000 passengers, and the total communications system linking air traffic controllers at La Guardia, Kennedy, and Newark airports.

The alarm bells at the 33 Thomas Street station rang unheeded for six hours. The AT&T personnel in charge of the rectifiers were away attending a one-day seminar on how to handle emergencies.[2]

Churches aren't always divided by a frontal assault on a matter of doctrine or practice. Sometimes it happens because everyone is so busy doing so many different things that they forget how important maintaining love and harmony is to the life of the church. Then, when the alarm bells ring, no one hears them—they're too busy.

Conclusion

God has a better plan for us than to spend our lives in anger toward other believers. His desire is for his will to be done on earth as it is heaven. That includes the principle, "Forgive us our debts, as we also have forgiven our debtors. And lead us not into temptation, but deliver us from the evil one" (Matt. 6:12-13).

For love and harmony to sweep through our churches, we must take these verses to heart. We must forgive those who wrong us, seek God's forgiveness for our own wrongdoing, and pray that we will be delivered from the schemes and designs of the devil.

Then the prayer Christ prayed for us on the last night of his earthly ministry can become a reality: "May they be brought to complete unity to let the world know that you sent me and have loved them even as you have loved me" (John 17:23).

It's not a question of whether your church will experience conflict, but will your church manage conflict in such a way that it survives the storm and emerges safely on the other side.

A pastor tells of an incident that took place in the days following the worst hurricane of the century in Florida:

A TV news camera crew was on assignment in southern Florida filming the widespread destruction of Hurricane Andrew.

In one scene, amid the devastation and debris stood one house on its foundation. The owner was cleaning up the yard when a reporter approached him.

"Sir, why is your house the only one still standing?" asked

the reporter. "How did you manage to escape the severe damage of the hurricane?"

"I built this house myself," the man replied. "I also built it according to the Florida state building code. When the code called for 2x6 roof trusses, I used 2x6 roof trusses. I was told that a house built according to code could withstand a hurricane. I did, and it did."[3]

If we build our relationships in the church according to God's design, then neither internal storms nor typhoons will be able to cause a collapse. Instead, when the storm has spent itself, we will be able to say, "We were told that a church built according to code could withstand a hurricane. We did, and it did."

May God's will be done on earth, as it is in heaven, and our love put into action.

Notes

1. Bill Hybels, "Standing in the Crossfire," *Leadership Journal* 14 (Winter 1993):14.

2. Phillip W. Gunter, "To Illustrate," *Leadership Journal* 14 (Winter 1993):48.

3. David R. Culver, "To Illustrate," *Leadership Journal* 14 (Winter 1993):49.